My Bo

Nyla Ditson

My Boaz, His Ruth

Cover photography: Shutterstock

For more information regarding permission to reproduce material from this book, please contact author at: www.facebook.com/booksbynyladitson & Nyla Ditson YouTube channel

ISBN:978-1-312-98491-2

Other Books by Nyla Ditson

Titles available on Amazon and Lulu books website, in eBook and paperback formats.

Angelic- A Christian fantasy novel about guardian angels and suicide not being the answer but God.

Blinded- A young summer love story about a girl recovering from an eating disorder who falls in love with a blind man.

Someone to Hold- A Christian romance story of falling in love with someone who later becomes famous.

Miracle Monday- Based on the true story of how a book was given to someone to save their life the night they planned to commit suicide.

"Focus on the benefits of singlehood, like being able to sleep in bed in your beloved star shaped position!"

- Pollyanna Oduesp

Chapter 1

"Work on becoming a woman worth waiting and fighting for. There are still amazing men out there, who are willing and eager to fight for you."

- **Highlighted from a commentary part in my Bible.**

"Why have a boyfriend when I can have a cat?"

I know what you are thinking: she's one of those single, crazy cat ladies! You probably have the same expression my best friend, Emily, has on right now. And like Emily, you may have snorted. Or perhaps scoffed when you read that line.

Let's be clear. I have *one* cat. I repeat, one cat! And technically, I only have half a cat. Wait! That sounds completely morbid. What I mean to say is, I *share* ownership to one feline. With my eighty-two year old grandfather. Cali lives with him at a senior's home and I shower her with affection and face nuzzles whenever I visit.

There is something different about you and Emily though, despite your similar reactions to my initial statement. Unlike you, she knows things about myself that I don't even know. And we've only been friends for three months.

"Lyndzi, pets are great but a relationship will happen when you're ready. When you've both learned the lessons individually God wants you to." Emily bends over and opens a cupboard, intent on filling the candy dishes up. It's Saturday, around ten am, on a sunny May morning. It's just the two of us in the frozen yogurt store, *Pure*. I'm sure in a few hours, around noon, we'll get some more customers. Some wanting something sweet, other's celebrating that university finals are over. "And what is it with you and cats lately?" she asks, standing, a frown and furrowed brow in place.

I take the large container of crushed Oreos from her and set it on the counter. "I miss Cali," I tell my black haired friend. "Only two more days and then I can cuddle with my furry friend again!"

Being a dog person herself, Emily rolls her eyes. But she's excited, even if she doesn't show it. Today's my second last shift, then we are carpooling home to Kindersley. I didn't grow up there like Emily's boyfriend did but my cousin, Cara Phelps, married a man from there. My aunt Jill, Uncle Randy and their teenage son, Jack, also live there. For the summer I'll be living at Cara's, working as a summer student for a local landscaping and gardening company, Gardening Galore. Bonus? Our grandpa recently relocated to Kindersley to live in the state of the art senior's home, Caleb Village. And with him? His beautiful calico cat, Cali!

For the next fifteen minutes, Emily and I silently work to fill the topping condiment bowls. From gummy bears, smarties, chocolate chips, rainbow sprinkles, fresh blueberries and raspberries, pineapple tidbits, shredded coconut, marshmallows and candied nuts, it's a sundae bar topping feast. Pretty much if you can think of it, we have it.

"Excited to spend time with your little cousins?" Emily asks, looking for a broom. Some shredded coconut got spilled on the floor from transferring it from the oversized container to the condiment bowl.

I nod. "Technically, Ruthie is my second cousin, but yeah, I'm pumped." I haven't seen Cara's ten month old since forever. I smile, just thinking of my cousin's adorable curly and dark haired daughter. Occasionally, I'll see family pictures posted on Facebook but it's not the same. You can't hear the giggle that's captured on camera or feel Ruthie's contagious energy. In their late twenties, Cara and her husband, Joey, are about six years older than me. I think Joey might be even a bit older. "And it will be great to see my grandpa more too."

The doorbell chimes as two teenagers walk in. They nod our way and make their way over to the frozen yogurt dispenser. Emily and I watch as they begin the near impossible challenge of deciding what flavour to get. Though we have some standard flavors, like vanilla and strawberry, we feature different speciality flavors every season. Right now, we have lemon meringue, turtle chocolate, sugar free raspberry crisp and mint fudge. I know, drool worthy and delicious, right? Brilliant marketing, if you ask me. Too many wonderful flavors to choose from equals people *not* deciding. Thus they take a bit of each and their personalized frozen yogurt becomes heavier.

"All ready to weigh it?" I ask as the teens come up.

They give me an odd look.

"Pretty sure they want toppings, Lyndzi," Emily laughs. "It's the best part."

"Right," I feel a blush. "My bad." *Man, I guess I'm more excited for summer to begin then I thought!*

The frozen yogurt shop is a fun place to work. Pretty funky decorating too, with its lime green walls, purple tables and colorful abstract pictures hung around in black frames.

Most of the pictures are composed of fruit and candy collages. But after working here since September, in between classes at the U of S, I'm ready for new scenery and schedule.

The rest of the day goes by fast. On average, we have six customers in the store at all times. Some pop in and out to get their sweet treat, some linger and chat at tables. There is a carefree feel to the air, especially when college age kids come in. Summer holidays, lack of studying and exams, has that effect. But with only a few months left of school for high school students and elementary kids, they seem extra happy too. Then again, maybe people are just happy in general around frozen yogurt. It's basically ice cream.

At ten pm, Emily and I perform our end of shift duties. I'm on autopilot, sweeping, refilling, moping the sticky floors by the yogurt dispensers, taking our red aprons to the laundry pile, checking cooler temps, sanitizing the tables and stainless steel counters, restocking the beverage cooler and doing the rest of my half of the chores.

"One more day and we are both done!" Emily says, flipping the open sign towards the building just before we lock up. "Then it's a whole new adventure awaiting us."

"Mmm, hmm." I slip the key into my pocket. Tomorrow I'm closing with a manager. I'll hand over my key to him then. "It's kind of sad, I liked this season of my life."

Our cars are parked next to each other. *Pure* is located in a strip mall in Lakewood, a quiet part of the city of Saskatoon. Nearby there's a coffee shop called Moka, a Boston Pizza, a fire fighter station, a Shoppers drug store and a few apartment buildings. Newly renovated Elim Tabernacle church is not too far away.

We linger by our cars, still wanting to chat, even though we will be seeing each other soon for the two hour drive to Kindersley come Monday morning. "Yeah, so did I," Emily admits. She loosens her black wavy hair from her messy bun. Understandably, we have to keep our hair tied back when working. Someone else's hair in your frozen yogurt would be beyond disgusting.

If I hȧd to associate Emily with a cartoon character, I'd pick Snow White. With her striking blue eyes, thin and defined face, milky white skin, silky dark hair, she could be hired to play the Disney princess at Disney land in a heartbeat. She also graceful, lean and long, with a tall dancer type body. Me on the other hand? I'm more curvy with more average height and features, light brown hair longish hair, slightly tanner skin then Emily, a few freckles (much darker now that it's sunnier), and hazel eyes. My smile is what people comment on most.

I chuckle. "Remember when that guy complimented me on my teeth?"

"Miss, do you know you have extraordinary teeth?"

"Or what about the customer who left then came back to compliment me on my beautiful teeth?"

Emily unlocks her car. "It's weird, complimenting someone specifically on their teeth. Saying they have a beautiful smile is different."

"Agreed. Less creepy." Our conversation lulls, signalling we are both tired from standing for a twelve hour shift and from cleaning in-between rushes. "I meant what I said though," I tell Emily, opening the door of my car. "About the cat thing. Unlike *someone*, I can't seem to find an amazing guy. So I think I'll just become a nun."

I duck just in time as Emily throws her purse at me. "Lyndzi! Brandon and I already explained this to you! Your life as a nun would *not* be how Whoopi Goldberg makes it out to be in *Sister Act.*" A nose scrunch. "Less exciting and... musical."

I pretend not to hear her. "It's a shame my parents didn't name me something that started with an N. Like Nancy or Nelly." Emily's eyes bulge. A look of confusion. I am used to getting this reaction from her. "So I could have a lovely alliteration. Nancy the Nun? Beautiful sound."

Emily and I met at a yoga class at the university gym in the fall and stuck up a conversation before class. Having a shared Christian faith, love of fitness and similar sense of humor, we were instant friends. Sometimes I still shock her with what comes out of my mouth. It's her fault, really. That I feel so comfortable to be my silly *and* my serious self with her. To be comfortably and unapologetically my unique personality, quirks and all. Not everyone in my life am I that at ease with. "The things that come out of that mouth of yours, Lyndzi. Maybe this is why you can't find a guy," Emily teases, leaving her car door open and walking towards me to retrieve her purse off the pavement. "You are aware that even if you were named Nancy, you wouldn't have your dream alliteration name."

I frown. "Yes, I would."

"No, you would be called *sister,* and you would then have to pick out a biblical name." A beep on her phone. From the type of smile on her face, I know it's Brandon, The Boyfriend. We are all pretty close. He's moving to Kindersley for the summer too, to work for the same company as Emily and I. It's going to be an awesome summer. "I better go, I need to get gas tonight still."

"Are you coming with Brandon or me to church tomorrow?" I normally go to a different church and they have been attending Elim, the one near work. From where I stand, I can see the large white church. Even in the dark night, it looks vividly bright. Like the moon or stars do, come onset of darkness.

"I think I'll go with Brandon tomorrow."

We say our goodbyes and get into our cars. I fiddle with my CD player, skipping ahead to find a song I'm in the mood to sing along to on the twenty minute drive home. "Alliteration dream shattered? Nah, just have to change the dream a tad. Hmm, Sister Sally? Nah, Sister Sandra?" I grin. That one I like. Makes me feel like Sandra Bullock. *Love her. She's a power woman in* Miss Congeniality *and a bunch of other movies...*

A knock on my window.

I jump, my seatbelt pulling tight against my chest. "Emily!" I close my eyes and put a hand to my heart. I hear her laughing even before I manually roll the window down. "Don't do that to me! You know I scare easy."

"That's why I do it often." She waits.

So do I. For what, I don't know. "Did you forget something? Change your mind about church?" I finally ask.

"No." I raise an eyebrow, giving her my best questioning look. A sigh and her smile slips slightly. "You know how I sometimes know things, that I typically shouldn't be able to know?"

A few months ago Emily revealed that God has given her a special gift, the Spiritual Gift of Knowledge. All Christians have a Spiritual Gift, some are more common, some rare.

Emily got one of the rare ones. "Yeah, is there something God told you about me?"

Her eyes darken. "Yes. I wasn't sure at first if I should tell you, but I think I'm supposed to."

I'm really curious now. "So spill, what is it?"

Her smile returns. "God told me you're going to get married and showed me who."

My mouth hangs open, very unlady like. I try to form word. The English language deserts me.

"No sisterhood for you!" Emily grins then runs back to her car. By the time the word "but" is on my lips, she's already pulling out of the parking lot, waving.

Gulp. *This is could get interesting.*

Chapter 2

"Enjoy your single years and all the benefits! They won't last forever."

- **Something my mom always said when I made a negative comment about being dateless yet again on a Friday night or a February 14th.**

Emily ignores all my texts that night and Sunday. Well, most of them. It's like she has selective texting, only answering the parts she wants too. Parts about confirming when we are leaving on Monday or about my questioning how many pants and shoes she is bringing.

"You can't just say something like that and leave!" I text her for the seventy-second time. Maybe I exaggerate slightly, but it feels like I've been screaming the same statement over and over, no response whatsoever.

"How would you like it if I did that to you, Emily!"

"What's he look like? Tall? Blond? Do I know him? Is he from Saskatoon? In his early twenties like us? Do *you* know him? Emily!!! Answer me!"

Her revelation in the parking lot changes things. Not our friendship but my pursuit. For him. For my future boyfriend and husband. What if she tells me his name? What if he annoys me? What if he's dating someone else right now? What if I'm not attracted to him? What if..... "Stop!" I tell myself. "You'll have her cornered in all four walls of a car for two whole hours, in less than twenty four hours. You'll get answers then." But something good does come from it: relief. From the pressure that I may end up as a true cat lady, living alone for life.

A beep from my phone. "Lyndzi, relax. Please don't stress about what I said," is what the text says.

My fingers furiously fly across my phone touch screen. So fast I have to backspace and fix multiple spelling errors. A few mistakes wouldn't be bad but over half misspelled words made for a jibberish but very amusing looking text. "RELAX!!!" I send in all caps, once I've fixed the spelling. "DON'T TELL ME TO DO IMPOSSIBLE THINGS!" I wait a full and extremely painful five minutes. But again, no text back. "On Monday, you're all mine," I tell my iPhone screen. "All mine."

By the time Emily pulls up outside my apartment Monday morning, I am more than ready for our chat. I don't wait for her text announcing her arrival. Neither do I allow her enough time to help me with my bags. I've already locked up and piled all my suitcases on my front patio. I've been waiting for her for the last twenty minutes.

"Do you need help?" she asks, watching, half amused, half concerned.

"What's that? Do I need answers? Why yes, I in fact do! Glad you asked!" I fling my bags into her opened car trunk, squishing my bags around her suitcases.

She sighs. "I should have never told you."

I place my backpack with my runners tied by the laces to it in the back seat. Then I join her in the car. Slipping on my seatbelt, I shake my head. "No, it's good that you did. A secret of such magnitude could make you fill with unhealthy secrecy, likely causing you to combust into chunks of dismantled human." I look over at her. The keys are paused mid-air, on their way to the ignition. "And no one likes a friend that does that."

A second later she shakes her head. "I'm not even going to respond to that." She's not mad, just tired. Aside from overtime days, we are both used to working the two to ten shift, meaning we can sleep in to noon, even on work days. Her black waves are tied back in a ponytail, with French braiding weaved down the side. A university grey bunny hug and sweat pants make up her assemble. Me? I'm no more fashionable. Hair in a messy bun, navy sweat pants material capris and purple tank top. It may still be cool out, it's technically not spring yet, but I'm one of those people who overheat fast. "What is this hour before noon?" I joke as we pull out from the curb.

Emily shrugs. "A cruel, cruel thing." She doesn't have to ask if I want coffee but stops at the Tim Horton's nearest my house. We go inside and grab mochas, bottled water and muffins for the drive.

I give her the full twenty minutes to the outskirts of the city until I pounce again. We've talked about when Brandon is driving up in two days, how we are looking forward to working outside all day for work, how it's so nice not to have the guilt of "I should really be studying" hanging over us, and how the second year of nursing was a lot more demanding than our first. Now it's time for even more riveting issue.

My future man.

"So, I'm not going to be a nun anymore, it seems." I say as we pass the Walmart at the edge of the city.

Emily shoulder checks and pulls in to the fast driving lane. "I can't answer everything you texted me, Lyndzi," she says, sounding apologetic. "But I might be able to give you some answers."

"Why do you get to know details that I can't? It's my life, my husband."

"Sometimes God reveals things to me, not to tell the person, but so I can know how to pray for them, how to prepare them for what is to come."

I think about this for a moment. A very God thing to do, giving her insight not just for the sake of handing out information. I suddenly think of something. "How did He tell you?"

She turns on cruise at exactly 110 km per hour and then points to her mocha. "Can you open that for me?" I pop the plastic part of the brown lid open, allowing the steam to release. "Thanks," she says as I hand it to her. After blowing on it, she takes a sip. It's painful, how long it's taking her to answer but I know she is taking her time for a reason. To find the right wording. And possibly praying to get a sense if God wants this particular question answered. "I usually get either a face or a name of the future spouse," she tells me finally, setting her drink down into the cup holder under the radio.

I stare at her in disbelief but she doesn't see my expression of shock. I hadn't even considered this not being the first time something like this has happened. "Typically it happens in the form of a dream, which is what yours was. After I'll pray a bunch to see if it was just a dream or was really God communicating to me. It's been a vision, like a day dream, once before too. Reality pauses and I just see this scene playing in my head, completely unaware of where I am while I watch." She pause to take another sip of her drink and then looks my way. Seeing my expression of awe and intrigue, mixed in with terror, she gives me a sympathetic look. "A lot to take in, I know."

Spiritual Gifts are not always prominently talked about in church. It's only after being friends with Emily that I've learned more about them. Essentially they are supernatural abilities given to Christians, with the purpose of using them to tell people about God and how He can change their lives. And they are meant to be used to strengthen relationships with Christ already in place. After praying for God to reveal what gift I had, I think I have the Spiritual Gift of Encouragement. Every believer gets at least one, although your gift can change or be only powered in certain situations or with certain people. "Have you told any of those other people that God told you who they would marry?"

She shakes her head, eyes on the road. Usually I love watching the prairie fields and wide open bright blue skies as we drive, but I can't stop staring at Emily, captivated by her words. It's like something out of a science fiction novel. But deep down, I know every word is true. I just have that for sure feeling. "You are the first one I ever told, Lyndzi."

"Oh, thanks, I think."

She takes her eyes off the road for a second to meet my gaze. "What I saw might not become reality though. Just so you know."

"What do you mean?"

She takes a second to gather her thoughts, again choosing to take a sip of coffee instead of answering right away. "What God showed me was His best choice for you. In life, we are often told there is The One mate for us." She shakes her head, showing her thoughts on this concept. "But if that were true, how would my mom have married after my dad died? We are created to be compatible with multiple people. It's choosing a wise choice from a sea of unwise choices that is key."

I take my bran muffin from its paper bag and break off a chunk. "So the guy in your dream about me was a wise choice then?"

She signals to pass the slow driver in front of us. Once we are safely back in the right lane she nods. "He was a wise choice but also the best choice. But free will, from your end or his, may change things."

I'm quiet, letting it all sink in. "Did God give you a name or show you his face?" I ask remembering her comment from earlier.

"A name."

"So you don't know him?"

"Lyndzi!"

I sit up. "You do, you totally do!"

Emily pulls over to the side of the road, onto the gravel. Shutting the car off, she turns to face me. "Yes, I recognize the name. But it doesn't mean you would. We have both lived in different cities and circles, for most of our lives. And the guy could have a common name, maybe the person I think is him, simply shares his name." True, very true. Emily has only been living in Saskatchewan since this year. She transformed from the U of A, in Edmonton, for her second year of nursing. "I really can't tell you anything else," she says. "Do you understand?"

After a moment, I glumly nod. "Yeah."

She pulls back onto the highway and neither of us brings up the subject again. But that doesn't mean I'm not thinking about it constantly. *Would I actually want to know his name?* I find myself wondering over and over. *What if I meet someone with that name? I would probably start hanging around him, pushing myself on him, not allowing the love story to just naturally unfold. And what if it wasn't him? But since he had the right name, I just kept pursuing him, blinded by factors that he didn't have but are non-negotiable on my list for a husband? What if I totally missed a wise choice because I was distracted by him, thinking he was the one I would marry?*

My thoughts start to give me a headache. I take Emily up on her offer of extra strength Advil. Finding it in her purse, I take one just as we drive through the small town of Rosetown. We stop at the 7 11 for a bathroom break and buy some nuts and more water.

Back on the highway, we turn on the only radio station that we can get, Kindersley and surrounding area's Mix 104.9. As I sing along to Taylor Swift's newest pop hit, I get a feeling that this summer is going to be full of lessons learned.

And you know what they say about lessons: some you have to learn the hard way.

Chapter 3

"Find a compliment to yourself, not a clone"

- I underlined this sentence in the relationship book "The Sacred Search" By Gary Thompson, which I got for Christmas this year.

We arrive in Kindersley around noon. Ironically, the last thing we saw leaving Saskatoon is one of the first things we see approaching Kindersley: a Walmart. As the car slows to a stop at the first intersection in the town of five thousand, my new home for the next three months, I gather my things. My purse, my crumpled napkin, empty water bottles by feat and my shoes. Yes, I'm one of *those* people. I hate wearing shoes when driving. My feet are much happier to curl up under myself, perfectly content being squished against my butt.

I note the new hotels constructed since my last visit five years ago, and a few new restaurants. As we pass the train tracks, I'm glad the famer's field in-between the two sub-divisions of Kindersley, the main part and the other called Rosedale, is still intact. There is something relaxing about being able to walk to a Wheatfield, while still remaining in town. I imagine I'll be out some mornings walking before work, enjoying the quiet and the beautiful prairie town scenery.

Five minutes later, we pull up to Cara and Joey's house in Rosedale. It's right across the street from a church, where Joey is the lead pastor. "Thanks for the lift," I tell Emily, unbuckling myself.

"Anytime, girl." She gets out to help me carry my things in, joining me at the back of the car.

"Emily?" She looks up from bending inside the trunk. "Why did you get the Spiritual Gift of Knowledge and not me?"

A knowing look crosses her pretty features. "I don't tell a lot a people about my gift, but rather pray to use it wisely and tell those on a need to know basis." She hands me my duffle bag. "But you're not the first person to ask me that question."

I hitch my backpack onto my shoulders, glad for it so I can carry more things in at once. "Your gift just seems so much more useful then encouragement. How come I get the lame gift?"

This time she stops what she's doing and focuses completely on me, voice firm. "All the gifts are important, Lyndzi. And the Holy Spirit discerns who would use what gifts best."

"So you are saying I wouldn't be a proper advocate of the Spiritual Gift of Knowledge?"

A frustrated sigh. "All I know is that specific gifts are given to specific people for a reason. Some people might not use it wisely or might brag about the secrets and inside information they know about people's lives. 1 Corinthians 8:1 explains it good, saying knowledge puffs up but love builds up." She pauses, taking a breath. "I didn't ask for this gift yet was given it anyways. But it's not always so enjoyable to have."

I set down my suitcase, my arm getting tired. My ten lbs workout dumbbells are in that bag. "How so?

"All the gifts have pros and cons. Take yours, encouragement, for example." Emily waves her hands as she talks. "Some people will be overjoyed by your encouraging words or actions. Others, not so much. A negative reaction to your heart to uplift can be so hard to deal with." She turns back to the trunk and grabs more bags, setting them by the bumper. "For me, sometimes I learned things about people I wish I didn't. Or sometimes I get woken up at four in the morning to urgently pray for people."

"God tells you what to pray for?"

"Yeah and sometimes I'll be up for five hours praying on their behalf." Her voices grows gentle. "The gift you have is amazing. Yes, I walk into a room and God sometimes reveals things to me about strangers or He can give me glimpses of futures and pasts of my family and friends. But I can only use that knowledge for those that it applies to." She jabs a thumb at my chest. "But encouragement can be used on *all* people. It's a forever need, in everyday situations."

Huh. Never thought about it like that. "Do you know stuff about Brandon?"

"No. God tends to reveal needs and hurts of people closest to me but not him yet." She slams the truck down. "The closer we became as friends, you and I, the more things God told me about you. And sometimes I'll even just get a sense you are having a hard day and need some prayer or an encouraging text."

We walk up the front sidewalk to the white sided house with the navy door and shutters. The grass is freshly mowed and there are a few toys on the front step by the flower pots. "Did you ever wake up to pray for me?'

A smile answers my question.

"Sometimes you need a friend more then I need sleep," I quote Emily back to herself. That's what she would say to me when she came to work exhausted. She'd mumble a friend called in the night. Now I understand what she had actually meant. "What else do you know about me?" I think to ask when we get to the front door.

She sets down the bags and knocks on the door. I think she's tiring of the topic. Or more specifically, the attention I'm giving her because of it. "I don't always necessarily know things about you that you aren't aware of. More so things your overlook and maybe don't realize the importance of." She goes on to explain how one friend had an addiction to gambling but before that was addicted to cocaine. God helped free the guy from his chains and he would sometimes share his testimony at events. God revealed to Emily that the man was focusing too much on the freedom from the drug abuse and overlooking the power of God's healing and strength executed in the gambling addiction freedom as well. "So I told him that both were power parts of his testimony. Now he includes other parts, and in the process, he's able to connect with more listeners and their struggles."

I want to ask more but the front door opens, reveling my blond curly haired cousin, Cara. "You made it!" She has Ruthie on her hip. The baby grins at us, revealing two bottom teeth.

"Sure did." I gestured to Emily. "This is my friend, Emily. She's Brandon Wake's girlfriend."

Joey comes up beside his wife, wearing his usual cheerful grin. I'd forgotten how tall my cousin's dark haired husband was. 6'3, at least! "Ah, Brandon. I miss that kid. Use to teach him piano lessons." Joey reaches out his hand towards us. "It's a pleasure to meet you, Emily. Welcome to our home and to Kindersley.

My friend holds out her hand, expecting Joey to take it. It takes a moment for Emily to realize Joey s blind. She quickly closes the distance. "Thanks, I'm excited to spend my summer here."

"Summer seasons in Kindersley can be quite memorable," Cara says in a reminiscing kind of way.

I've heard her and Joey's summer romance story before. How they met and fell in love in this very town, when they were around my age of twenty-two. Back then, Cara was extremely self-conscious of her looks but God used Joey and his blindness to teach Cara to look at herself differently. I'll have to fill Emily in on the details. Too bad she isn't staying with me at Cara and Joey's place. *I could go for a late night gab fest tonight.* But she is staying at Brandon's in their guest room. It will be a good way for her to get to know his family. They've been dating six months, I do believe. This will be only the second time she's met his folks.

After Emily helps haul my things into the guestroom on the main level, I wave goodbye to her and then say hello to my new living quarters. The next few days are spent settling in, biking around the town, playing with little Ruthie, asking Cara about her current pregnancy, helping make meals and gathering around the piano with Ruthie, Cara and Joey to listen to the male of the family serenade us with his God given talent of piano playing. Even after his university basketball accident, that cost him his eyesight, his passion for music and resilient spirit helped him learn to play again. Often he'll do special music and be the main pianist at church. And to the best of my knowledge, I think he's still giving piano lessons in his free time.

“First day of work tomorrow,” Cara comments on Wednesday night, after coming back to the living room after putting Ruthie to bed. “Excited?” She makes herself comfortable on the couch, cozying up beside Joey on the couch. He puts an arms around her and one on her round belly.

I set down my glass of pink lemonade on the coffee table, enjoying the sight of them but aching for my own love story at the same time. “Yeah, kind of. I’m glad Brandon and Emily will be working with me.” I see a wedding photo album on the table and pick it up. I run my thumb over the black and white cover photo. Aside from looking a bit older, Joey and Cara look the same as they did on their wedding five years ago. Cara’s natural ringlets are maybe a bit longer now but Joey’s hair is just as wavy and windblown looking as it is in the picture. Both are gazing into each other’s eyes in the photo, fully in love, fully ready for life to be an adventure for two.

“Did you guys ever wonder about who you were going to marry, before you met each other?” I set the photo album down and turn my attention to the couple beside me on the couch.

“Sometimes,” Cara nods. “But I was really focused on my appearance so the hope of finding love wasn’t prominently on my radar.”

It’s as if Joey knows my gaze has come to him. He answer right on cue, turning his bright blue eyes towards me. They are focused slightly off of my eyes but I know he’s doing his best to keep eye contact.” I thought about my future wife a ton,” he confesses. “Wondering when we would cross paths, if we had already, that sort of thing.”

"So what did you do?" I inch closer, as if being physically nearer will make the answers come quicker.

Joey takes his arms off his wife, muscular from rowing and weightlifting, as his hilarious stories during supper about spinach and Popeye not living up to the hype of making you strong had mentioned. He leans over Cara's bulging stomach. "I talked to my dad and he told me, 'Son, focus on becoming the person you are looking for is looking for."

Whoa. Deep.

"Didn't another pastor say that?" Cara asks, standing. She arches her back, hand on the small of her back. "I feel like I've watched a YouTube sermon on that back in my university years." Cara's a teacher now and earned her teaching degree where I now study, at the University of Saskatchewan.

Joey stands to join his wife. "Yeah, Andy Stanley has a serious on that topic, called *The New Rules for Love, Sex and Dating.* My dad must have watched it before our talk."

As I ready for bed that day, I muse over the quote. Pulling up the covers to my chin, I look out the window to the stars and wonder if my future husband and I were to meet tomorrow, would we both be the kind of people each other is looking for?

***

My first day of work comes and go. I don't end up working with Emily or Brandon. Though I did see them back at the main office building during our lunch break. It was nice to swap stories of the day. Maybe another day we will be assigned jobs together. Today we were sent to different jobs. Brandon spent the day on a ride on mower, cutting the large grassy areas of the schools. Emily was helping lay down sod at a person's house in Rosedale and I used up my eight hours hauling trees out of a backyard as another worker chain sawed them down. The work was tiring and dirty. But at least it isn't as hot as it will get eventually mid-summer. And my boss, Bob, is kind. Always reminding the crews, via radios in the company white trucks, to take snack breaks and water breaks as needed. It felt good biking back to Cara and Joey's after a long day, full of honest and hard earned wages. And don't even get me started on the shower after I got home! Dirt and twig free hair and skin feels divine.

"My arms sting," I complain at supper that evening. From her highchair, Ruthie cocks her head to one side. She is a combination of Cara's fair skin and curls and Joey's vivid blue eyes and dark brown hair. "Should have worn long sleeves, I guess!" I say to Ruthie, making a funny face. She giggles and smiles big, her chubby cheeks appearing even bigger.

Cara sets a bowl of homemade macaroni and cheese down on the table. Joey follows not far behind with a pot holder. Already a spinach salad, bread and butter, and peas and carrots are on the table.

We all hold hands and dip our heads as Joey says grace. I hold onto Ruthie's small sticky hand. *It's either apple juice or smushed banana I'm now experiencing as lotion.* As gross as it feels, I don't mind. Being around the Waterloo's, especially little Ruthie, is a delight. When the baby flashes me her toothy grin, smiles up at me, or shrieks with laughter at one of my goofy faces, my heart sores. Problems or tiredness don't seem so strong.

"Why did you name her Ruthie?" I ask, taking the bowl of peas and carrots Joey hands me. "Do we have someone in the family named that?"

"Don't think so," Joey and Cara reply at the same time. They laugh and then Cara explains. "We named her after Ruth from the Bible."

"Ah," I scoop a big helping of creamy noodles onto my plate. The melted cheddar cheese sticks to the spoon, the way stringy cheese from pizza often does. The sight of it makes me real excited. "Like Boaz and Ruth, that story?"

"That's the one," Joey answers, dishing himself up food. Although Joey is very independent, despite his disability, there are some things he can't do. Like feed a baby. Cara is attempting to feed Ruthie her supper of mashed vegetable and fruit concoction. It's comical watching Ruthie's facial expressions. "I thought you loved me!" Her face seems to say. "Why are you feeding me this awful textured stuff?" I want to mention her priceless look but don't. I don't want to make Joey feel bad about what humorous things he can't see.

Too my surprise, Cara does just what I decided not to. "Oh, Joey," she laughs. "I just have to describe Ruthie's face to you. She looks like I'm feeding her dog food!"

I laugh alongside Joey. Although Joey's Seeing Eye Dog, a golden retrieved named Mac, is great with kids, even he wouldn't be too thrilled about his supper being fed to an unappreciated baby.

Giving up on the cooked sweet potatoes, Cara moves onto dessert, a medley of mashed berries. Though she refuses at first, once she gets a taste of the sweet berries, Ruthie opens her mouth as wide as it can go. "This one likes her sweets, just like her dad," Cara comments, easily slipping spoonfuls of fruit into her daughter's mouth.

"Ice cream, best invention ever," Joey declares, wearing a fond look on his face. "You had my dream job, Lyndzi, working at an ice cream place. That's like heaven on earth."

"Frozen yogurt," I correct. "After a while you get sick of it though. I don't think I'll crave it ever again. Too many breakfasts, lunches and suppers consisted of frozen yogurt. As a student, that 50% off employee discount for food was too tempting!"

This earns me laughs. After supper winds down, Joey takes Ruthie into the living room. She's getting a bit cranky as its nearing her bath and bed time. Joey takes her to the piano and sets her on his lap. I watch as the child instantly cheers at the sound of her dad softly playing, "Somewhere Over the Rainbow" on the piano. Every so often she will reach down and bang one of the keys, eyes bright and excited at the discovery of being able to create sounds.

"I think someone is going to take after their dad," I say, turning my attention back to drying the dishes.

"Joey says he's the baby whisper," Cara smirks, handing me a clean plate. "But it's the piano."

"Too bad I didn't bring my guitar, I bet Ruthie would have loved that."

"I think Jack has one," Cara says, a thoughtful look on her pretty face. Pregnancy definitely has given her a joyful glow. Though I'm sure it's also a part of her strong faith. Beauty from within shining out. "I could ask him to bring it to church on Sunday."

"Sure, that'd be awesome." It would be great to see my other family too. Our cousin Jack lost his leg in a car accident at nine years old. But just like Joey, he didn't let the loss of a body part or ability keep him down. From Christmas newsletters and family reunions over the years, I know that Jack is as busy as any typical teenager. Last I heard, he was a starter for his high school basketball team, the Kindersley Kobras.

Fast-forward a few more days of eight to five work shifts, lots of dirt, sweat and sore muscles, I find myself sitting in church Sunday morning. My cousin Jack, with blond curls like Cara, sits next to me. At sixteen, he's already six feet and lanky. His parents are away camping so it's just him today at church.

Ruthie and Cara are in the nursery, as the eleven o' clock service falls right during one of Ruthie's typical feeding times. They should be back in a few minutes.

"Be nice to my girl," Jack whispers, nudging the black guitar case at his feet. "I know where you live."

I stifle a laugh. "You gave your guitar a gender?"

"And a name, Bonnie the Beauty." He scrunches up his face, one that will make many teenage girl's hearts lurch, if not already. With his humor, athleticism and looks, he probably had all the girl's attention from day one of high school. "Girlfriends come and go but guitars, they are forever."

A tanned blond in front of us turns and glares at Jack. "You know I'm sitting right in front of you, right?"

A sheepish look crosses Jack's face. "Sorry, Amanda. I didn't see you there."

She rolls her eyes. "I think some time apart would be good." *Oh, I wish I wasn't here. This feels awkward to be overhearing this.* I'm about to head to the nursery, to check on Cara when Amanda continues, putting both myself and Jack at ease. "From you *guitar*, Jack! Don't look at me like that. I'm not breaking up with you."
Jack wipes a hand across his forehead. "You nearly turned my curls grey!" He looks around quickly before leaning forward to kiss her forehead. "I'd love you even if you did though."

Blushing, Amanda turns away.

The worship team, consisting of a drummer, two acoustic guitarists and three singers get onto the stage and the congregation stands. Joey's at the grand piano, leading us in music for the next twenty minutes. As I sing, I think back to the sweet teenage love exchange I just witnessed. Yes, Jack has been through a lot, with his amputation and learning to cope, more than I had at his age...

But why does he get a love story before me?

I sing the songs but my heart isn't in it. It's not like I'm desperate for a boyfriend. I'm happy being single. I enjoy spending my Fridays and evenings how I want to, eating what I want, not having to always consider a second party in life decisions, small or big. Sure, I still take into consideration the consequences my actions have on others, but it would be different if I were in a relationship. *I just want someone to do life with. The movies and couples I know make it look enjoyable, though I know it will be like any friendships, requiring lots of time, effort and work.* I find great purpose, satisfaction and identity in being a Christian. So it's not like I think having a boyfriend would fix my life or make me happier. I'm perfectly content now. Well, sorta. There is a part of me that longs to have what others have, to have that connection with someone. To be chosen by someone to have forever with.

My thoughts are broken when Joey steps up to the pulpit. Unlike other speakers, he can't take sermon notes with him. A benefit of this is that he's never tempted to read straight from the page. I've heard him speak only a handful of times and he is really gifted at engaging the audience, like he's simply having a conversion with them.

"Today we are going to be looking at the book of Ruth," Joey opens up with just as Cara and Ruthie return to our pew. Setting her diaper bag down, Cara hands Ruthie to me. I take her so Cara can gather some toys and board books to keep Ruthie occupied.

I give Ruthie my bulletin and she instantly sticks it in her mouth. *Sometimes the most loved toys are the ones that don't cost a thing.* Seeing Ruthie content on my lap, chewing away at the bulletin, Cara raises an eyebrow. I nod, signalling I'm fine to keep her for the rest of the service. Or until she gets fussy. Whichever comes first. Relaxing, Cara leans back against the pew and settle sin to listen to Joey's sermon. As do I.

"Now the love story of Boaz and Ruth is a small but powerful one in the Bible." Joey leans on the side of the pulpit, voice animated. "Boaz came from a wealthy family, whereas Ruth did not. In fact, they even came from different countries." Joey goes on to explain how Ruth's first husband was killed so she traveled to her mother in law's (Naomi), old country, where they both lived as widows. "And cue Boaz," Joey chuckles. "He saw Ruth gathering wheat in his field one day, something that the poor were allotted to do."

Slowly, Joey makes his way down the front steps of the stage. I wonder if he's mentally counting the pews because he stops at ours. *Good thing Cara came back in time. I feel like this maybe wasn't planned.* But God clearly got Cara back in order to play a part in whatever was to come. And most likely the Waterloo family, like other families in the congregation, have a spot they typically sit on Sundays. *Probably how he knew where to stop.* "Most of you are aware that my wife and I named our first child Ruthie, after the biblical character."

Sensing I'm supposed to hand her over to Joey, I stand and give Ruthie to him.

Nodding his thanks, Joey then looks adoringly down at his daughter. She is mimicking the loving gaze, still slobbering all over the bulletin. "We did this not only to remind her of the godly character traits to strive for found in Ruth in this story, but also in Boaz. To remind her one day that she is worth waiting for a Boaz, not a Bozo, to pursue her and win her heart. When a man has to fight for your heart, and work for it, he'll keep fighting to keep it later in life." Joey looks my way, even though I'm not sure how he could possibly know where I'm sitting. But I have a sense it's like Emily, and God simply directs Joey where to look in this moment.

Joey holds Ruthie out and Cara takes her. Moving back to the front, he continues his sermon from the pulpit. He shares how Ruth was in Boaz's field for a purpose because Naomi wanted Boaz to notice Ruth. Naomi knew he was a solid godly man and wanted Ruth in his care. I listen intently to the familiar Bible story, how Boaz showed compassion for Ruth, how he was attracted to her faithfulness to her mother law and her hard and honest work ethic, how he told his workers to protect Ruth and leave extra wheat for her and how eventually they wed, so Boaz could take care of Ruth and Naomi. He shares that the qualities we wish to see in others, we must give ourselves a honest "heart check" and see if we possess them ourselves. To be the friend we wish we had for ourselves to others, to be the spouse and significant other we would appreciate.

"Look for a Boaz and be his Ruth," I whisper to myself that night in bed, staring at the ceiling. It was kind of a paraphrased version of what that Andy Stanley quote about focusing on possessing the character traits that the person you were looking for would find attractive. Things they would be drawn to if they were to walk into the room today. I flip over to my side. *Easier said than done sometimes, especially in the season of waiting.*

But like Emily, my mom and Cara and Joey keep saying, there must be a reason for the waiting. God wouldn't keep him from me just to be cruel.

Chapter 4

"On the lonely nights, pray and write letters to your future spouse. Before you say I do, ask yourself, will this person cherish the words I penned to them before we met? Can I comfortably give them these recorded glimpse of my heart?" Present the letters to them on your wedding night.

- **Cara told me this during one of our late night chats. Conveniently, I was up getting water while she was feeding Ruthie.**

"Nice jeans," I compliment Emily as I park my bike next to hers and Brandon. Her dark jeans are strategically and stylishly ripped at the knees. With supper and work behind us for the day, we planned to go for a bike ride around the town walking trail.

Emily stands from where she and her Brandon are sitting on a nearby bench, waiting for me to arrive. Always a few minutes late, this one! "Thank you! At least someone appreciates them," she says, shooting Brandon her Look of Death.

I cast her a quizzical look.

Brandon rolls his eyes, standing to join us by the bike rack. "I will never make that mistake again, I swear." Truly a hipster, he is. With his love of those slouchy toques, his assortment of colorful skinny jeans, multiple ear piercings (some of those ear stretching ones too) and band t-shirts. Not to mention his oversized black glasses.

I unclip my white helmet chin strap, wondering what poor thing the blond spiked hair, tanned and brown eye boy in my presence must have said. "Emily?" I ask when it's apparent Brandon isn't going to elaborate.

"Said he could help me out on a pair of new jeans, if I was short on cash."

My helmet dangling by my side, I burst out laughing. "That's like the time that one professor tried to remove your Lululemon brand mark from your pants, thinking you had a sticker stuck on." Brandon and I chuckle, remembering how annoyed Emily had been for the remainder of the day after her psychology class.

"I paid mega bucks for that brand name and he tried to take it off!" Emily shakes her head, clearly still miffed at the memory.

We grab our bikes, Emily and mine borrowed from our billets for the summer, and begin biking. It's a perfect temperature evening. A slight breeze but warmer enough for my jean shorts and striped white and pink tank top. A heavy layer of mosquito spray was also a good call, I think as I accidently swallow one. "That was not an enjoyable experience for either one of us," I spit out, pulling my bike over.

Emily and Brandon stop at the top of the hill, looking over their shoulders at me. "How was work today for you, Lyndzi?" Brandon calls out. I have yet to work with him, after a week and a half passed since our first day.

I wipe my mouth and then press off my back petal, catching up to them quickly. "Not bad. Emily got the short end of the stick I think though."

She's at the front, her long black hair down and flowing from her helmet. "This is true!" she calls out, overhearing my comment.

Whereas my day was spent in a combination of weeding various gardens, buying some flower bulbs at Walmart for a flower display, wiper snipping and removing some gravel from a yard, Emily's *entire* day was spent at the gravel job, shoveling.

"I hate gravel!" was what she texted me after work. "Loath it to death."

As we bike around the 3km loop, I marvel at the beauty of our surrounding. There are tall evergreen trees, overgrown shrubbery, a wide paved path, various log picnic tables and benches and a large man-made lake in the center. It's a breathtaking place to relax after a long day. Even though we can't chat for long, since we are mostly biking in a single line and at slightly different speeds, it's still nice to be good company, experiencing a shared enjoyable activity. Even better, we seem to be the only ones on the trail tonight, aside from one dog walker.

Approaching a red steel bridge, we stop and take a moment to savor the view of the water and the other side of the trail from across the water.

"My jeans cost me well over a hundred dollars," Emily comments, turning to Brandon and me, still perched on our bikes beside her.

"These," Brandon points to his grey shorts, "hand-me-downs."

"Translation: already worn in and beautifully free!" This earns me a huge grin and a high-five from him.

"Frays are like flaws, you guys," Emily says, smiling at our exchange. I'm glad I don't feel like a third wheel with them. It's because of me that Brandon even met Emily in the first place. He and I were on a water polo team at the university. When I mentioned I worked at *Pure* after one game, he decided to stop by, thus meeting Emily. I may have introduced them then *I may have* spilled my bucket of soapy mop water so Emily had to serve him and not me. *Clever matchmaker, if I do say so.*

"I'm all for accepting flaws," Brandon says. "If people didn't, I wouldn't have a great girl like you, Em."

"Brandon, might want to reword that!" I tell him turning my bike away from the steel bridge and back to the path. "She could take it two ways!"

"Oh!" I hear him exclaim behind me. "I meant you were the one accepting a flawed person! Not me!"

I leave them alone, gaining speed on the trail. They haven't worked together much yet either. Even though they are living in the same house, it's nice to have some time alone.

There are about thirteen of us on the gardening crew. We meet each day at eight at the main office. We change into our overalls and steel toes, get our assignments for the day, gather our equipment and break into various work trucks to go to our job sites around the town. Yes, we get to chat before the boss gets there, at lunch and our breaks, but I still wish I'd get to spend a full day working with Brandon and Em. It's what I envisioned when I applied for the job. Still, the season is young. And it's given me opportunity to get to know the other summer students I have been regularly teamed up with better.

As I bike solo, loving the feel of flying down the windy trails, occasionally looking to my right to the water, I think back to Emily's comment about flaws. *I'm not looking for a perfect man. So maybe he isn't either. I don't want a prefect body or character, that's not attractive. I want someone real.*

A conversation comes to mind, one I shared with a friend over Starbucks. We'd been discussing a book we both read, called "A Man Worth Waiting For" by Jackie Kendall

"What did you think about the part about flaws?" Gwen had asked me, sipping her green tea frappuccino.

I lowered my venti raspberry iced tea. "It was an eye opening way to look at it. I liked how the author said not to look for a flawless man but rather look at how he handles his flaws. Does he use them as a reminder to draw closer to God? To grow his character by learning from lessons? Or does he turn to unhealthy things, like anger, blaming or unhealthy habits with alcohol or TV?"

Interesting, I muse, reaching the start of the trail first. As I wait for Emily and Brandon, I gaze across the water, focusing on the appearing light pinks and oranges of the sunset. *Another item to add to my marriage and relationship tool box.*

I hear them before I see them. They are clearly racing. I hop off my bike, cheering them on. But all the while I'm thinking about a new concept. *I'm glad I've learned some things before I've met him.* And I have a feeling that my toolbox will be even fuller, gaining new and invaluable insights that myself and my future significant other will be so grateful I learned prior to crossing paths. Maybe, just maybe, Emily had it right. There was a reason for the waiting.

A darn tootin' good reason.

***

It rained the next day so the entire crew spent the day cleaning. It was nice, getting to interact with Emily and Brandon throughout the days. Since grass can't be nicely cut when wet, the push mowers, hedges, weed whackers, chainsaws and the various sized ride on mowers were all blown off, washed and had oil changes. The work trucks got a good cleaning, vacuumed, straightened up inside, washed, gassed up and polished.

"I'm heading out to see Grandpa," I tell Cara, coming out of my room, hair still wet from my shower, post dinner.

"I wish I could come with you," she glances at the clock. "But Ruthie needs to start her bath in twenty minutes."

I hold up my hands. "Please don't mess with bath and bed routine! We will all pay the price!" I'm half joking. Ruthie hasn't been too loud in the night. But that kid can get crabby in the day when she's overtired.

After promising to say hi to our grandpa, I leave. I wave to Joey, meeting him on the sidewalk outside the house. He's just coming home from work, across the street at the church. Remembering he can't see my greeting, I add a verbal hello. "Hey, Joey. How was work?"

He loosens his green tie. "Pretty good, expect I found out the person slotted for special music on Sunday isn't going to be there now. I played and sang piano the last three weeks. I was looking forward to having someone different this week."

Not really thinking about it, I offer to help. "I could do it." I'm not the most talented guitarist but I know enough chords to get through a song. And I'm told my voice is pretty.

"Maybe an old hymn? Something that I've already played numerous times so I don't have to practice much beforehand?"

Joey's eyes lit up. "That would be awesome, Lyndzi!" He hugs me and I'm still laughing as I walk the five blocks to Caleb Village.

I enter the building through the automatic double doors, sign in at the front desk and then press floor three in the elevator. "You know you're on the right level if the walls are blue," the receptionist had told me, explaining all the floors are painted a different color so the elderly residents can easily tell if they are on their proper floor.

Stepping out of the elevator, I see blue walls so I head to room 205. There is a picture of Grandpa on the door, as there were photos of each room's occupants that I passed on the way.

I knock and then let myself in. Grandpa's expecting me. "Hello?" I call out, walking into the kitchen area.

"Lyndzi! Come here, my girl!" My grandpa rises from the couch, his love of *Wheel of Fortune* nothing in comparison to seeing me. Seeing his favorite show on the television, I know we'll be watching a bit of it together during our visit. It's something we've often done and I'm glad this summer we will get to do it more.

Grandpa wraps me into his arms. He's shorter than me so I rest my head on his shoulder. He's warm and smells of mint leaves and bounce laundry sheets. I don't even have to look to know that there will be peppermint candy tray on his table somewhere. Pink or white, he was always offering the grandkids and cousins them at family visits to his old home.

After our hug, he shuffles back to his couch. He's plumper then the last time I saw him. *The cooks at Caleb must be to his liking.* But his hair is the same, white and combed over, Donald Trump style. And his smile? Just as kind and loving as always.

"So we are town mates for a while!" Grandpa smiles, revealing his dentures are in place.

"So it seems," I sit next to him. "How do you like it here?" He's been here only a couple of months. After Grandma suddenly passed away last year, from a broken hip turned into pneumonia, he just couldn't keep up the house on his own in Kerrobert. It's a town about forty-five minutes away from Kindersley. Some aunts live there but he has more care and family here in Kindersley and at Caleb.

"They serve ice cream here every afternoon," Grandpa tells me. "And a snack cart comes by too, with chocolate bars and other goodies."

"You and your sweet tooth." I shake my head, smiling. My grandpa is not one of those elderly people who eat like a bird. No, he'll eat as much as my dad then ask for seconds of dessert. Grandma used to limit his diet but if the extra pounds on his short frame are any indication, the staff at Caleb are all for more desserts.

"Hey! Where's Cali?" I look around for the precious calico cat. Without asking my parents, I adopted her at a garage sale. Not having the heart to tell their seven year old that she couldn't have a cat, because her brother had allergies, my parent's asked my grandparents to take the cat. After fourteen years of seeing Cali throughout the years rather often, the cat with mostly white with ginger, brown and grey patches knows me. She's still as friendly and cuddly as ever. She's definitely slowing down and not as energetic as the kitten version of Cali.

"Over there," Grandpa points to the chair by the patio door. *Typical Cali, always sleeping in the sunniest part of the house.* I don't want to move her, she's smiling in her sleep.

We chat about life at Caleb, the other residents that regularly sit at Grandpa's table downstairs for the meals, the special music and games nights throughout the week, the bible study he attends with some other men in the building on Thursdays and the hymn sing on Sunday afternoon. Eventually Cali wakes, stretches and then hops off her chair.

"Meow!" she says, sitting on her hind legs before me.

"Meow to you too," I say, scooping her up. She immediately starts purring and rubbing her face against mine. We cuddle and I realize just how much I have missed these two. After we all watch the last half of *Wheel of Fortune*, Grandpa turns the TV off, a sly look on his face.

Oh, no. I know where this is going. He's definitely my father's father. That's the same look Dad wears when he asks about my love life.

"Got a male companion these days?"

I start picking at my chipped black painted nails. "Sadly, no."

Grandpa removes a peppermint from his pocket. "Aww, that's too bad. You're a godly woman, Lyndzi. A catch worth waiting for."

I take the peppermint from him, not surprised he has a secret stash in his wool sweater vest pocket. "Did you ever wonder when you would meet your wife?" I wish I could ask Grandma a similar question.

Grandpa is quiet, starting at the dark TV screen. "My life had April in it longer then it didn't. It's hard to think back to my days before her."

My heart sinks. I was hoping to get some great advice from him.

"But if I remember correctly, your grandma mentioned something similar in a journal entry of hers." He eases himself slowly from the couch and moves towards his bedroom. A few minutes later he emerges, an old looking coil style notebook in hand. "I've been reading it lately, on the nights where missing her gets to be too much."

I hug my grandpa, wondering how people can love so deeply and then live after a loss. *It must feel like losing a limb.* "I'm sorry, Grandpa. I'll be praying for you. That God continues to comfort you."

He wipes at his eyes, hazel like mine. We are the only ones in the family with that unique coloring. It's actually one of my favorite features of myself. Sometimes they appear brown and in other lights the green and gold flecks are picked up. "The Good Lord has comforted me much, Lyndzi. I keep dreaming of my April in heaven, dancing with The Lord and singing her favorite hymns."

"I know Caleb has a service on Sundays, but would you like to come to Joey and Cara's church this Sunday?" I explain that I'm doing a special music. "And I think I know which song I'll do now. Grandma's favorite hymn."

He gets a whimsical look on his face, as if remembering when his bride would sing it as she did dishes or cleared the table. How she sounded singing it with the choir on Sundays or to her children before bed. “Great is Thy Faithfulness.”

After promising to pick him up at ten-thirty on Sunday and petting Cali one final time, I leave, taking the notebook with me. There is a sidewalk, about a block and half long between the church and Caleb Village. I plan to meet Grandpa in the lobby and walk with him to the church.

Once I get back home, I glance at my watch. It’s just about nine. Still time to do something before bed. I say hi to Joey and Cara, cuddled on the couch, watching the news, bowls of ice-cream in their hands. I know Joey listens to the TV but from the look on his face, I think he’s concentrating harder on his late night dessert.

“Want some?” Joey asks looking up, sensing me standing near the couch.

“No, thanks. But Grandpas tells me they serve it often at Caleb. We should join him for lunch there sometime.”

Cara licks her bowl clean of vanilla ice-cream, chocolate sauce and smarties. “I’ve lost count of how many times we’ve been there, over ice-cream hour.” She jabs Joey in the side. “This one takes his coffee breaks over there, sometimes coming home too full for supper.”

We decide to join Grandpa for lunch on Sunday after church. It’s been a while since he’s seen Ruthie. I’ll phone Grandpa and confirm tomorrow. “I’m going to go outside for a bit,” I tell them. “Call me in before you go to bed.”

They nod and I go to my room. Grabbing a lightweight grey bunny hug, I slip it on, put my moccasins on, grab Jack’s guitar from the case and then tuck Grandma’s old journal under my arm. Once I’m outside, I sit on the step of the patio, overlooking a spacious laws. There is a lawn edging and bark around the yard with various trees and decorated pots. A white fence surrounds the perimeter.

Finding my guitar tuned, it's the first time since I've played it since borrowing it, I pluck away at the chords for "Great is Thy Faithfulness". The version I know is easy, only six different chords. I quietly sing, watching the twinkling stars as I do. "Great is thy faithfulness... strength for today and bright hope for tomorrow, blessings all mine with ten thousand behind." I'm mixing up the chorus and the verses. I'll have to Google the lyrics on my laptop before Sunday. Even mixed up, I feel encouraged and connected to God through the words.

Sighing, I set down the guitar. Pulling my iPhone from my jean pockets, I use the flashlight app to ultimate the yellowed pages of my Grandma April's journal.

"Somewhere near the end, she wrote a piece about waiting for me to arrive." Grandpa's eye had grown full of love this afternoon, at the mention of his beloved wife. "The date it was written was nearly two years before we met at the fair." He'd assured me he had many of her other journals to read, to keep him company with her memories and words late at night when sleep wouldn't come.

I flip the book open. For the next thirty minutes, I get a glimpse into my grandma's heart. Her dreams, desires, fears, triumphs and trials. Some people may feel like they are invading privacy by reading such intimate things like a diary. But I have a gut feeling that my grandma wouldn't mind. She'd want her journals to be used to encourage and equip me.

A section close to the back catches my eye, because of the words "Waiting for the Man of my Prayers."

Bingo. Just the topic of my particular interest. I settle against the wooden step, excited and curious to read if anything my grandma has written will be relevant to me today, in my pursuit and waiting period for my godly man.

February 11th, 1946

"I bet they'll be engaged by the end of the year," I think after observing my good friend and her boyfriend.

"Look what I got for Christmas!" an acquaintance showed me the other day, shoving the stunning diamond ring on her hand near my face. And during the holidays, four couples got engaged from my young peoples' church group.

With Valentine's Day and a family reunion approaching, where babies, boyfriends, girlfriends and other new additions are introduced to the family, I find myself thinking about him more often. The young man I will walk down the aisle towards someday. The one who will be nervous meeting my parent's for the first time. The man who gives me The Look, where he looks at me like I'm the most beautiful girl he's ever seen and can't believe I'm his. That him.

"Where are you? Why is it taking us so long to find each other?" I mutter sometimes, irritated that he's being a slow poke. Even if I truly do love parts of my singlehood.

Lately, I've been doing a lot of research on relationships. Mostly through talking to older couples in my life about how to maintain godly dating and marriages. Conversing with them is giving me tools to take into a relationships but it's also scaring me! How am I supposed to remember to apply all these concepts into my life? I'm forgetful and flawed!

"Don't worry," I heard God whisper to me recently. "There is reason for this waiting, April."

"How so?" I asked in my heart.

"You're not ready yet, as your anxieties are showing. Through this time apart, I'm equipping you with the tools to participate in the godly relationship of your dreams."

"Oh. Thanks for the waiting then!"

I picture God smiling, His eyes twinkling. "My pleasure, April."

So why the wait for the man of my prayers? Put simply, we aren't ready. God isn't going to throw me into a situations without preparing me first. What relief! I am ever grateful He doesn't listen to my inpatient prayers! I see the present, He sees eternity. I see a part and He sees a whole.

This time apart is invaluable, teaching us both individual lessons that we can then bring to our relationship. God clearly still wants to keep molding us into different people before He crosses our path.

I do believe he's out there. A few weeks ago, I was praying at school, that one day God would bring a man worth waiting for into my life. A gentleman, but a fierce protector. Someone who loves Jesus with as much enthusiasm as I do. Someone who loves talking about his faith, like I do. Someone who challenges me but also needs my wisdom and support.

So, if you're waiting for something, a spouse, a new job opportunity or guidance for a life changing decision, just keep waiting. There is reason in the waiting. Take Elizabeth, from the Bible. She and her husband, Zechariah, prayed for children and yet Elizabeth remained barren for years. But then, in her old age, God blessed them with a child. During the same time that Elizabeth's younger cousin, Mary, was pregnant with her first child, Jesus! Because of the waiting, Elizabeth and Mary got to share in the thrill and fear of a first time pregnancy together. They spent a few months together, encouraging and experiencing life with one another. What a precious gift! Previously, Elizabeth may have thought God wasn't answering her prayers. But He was just whispering a quiet, "Wait, Elizabeth. Through waiting, your prayers with be answered in a much more beautiful way."

God doesn't delay answering prayer to be unkind. Sometimes if we were to get what we prayed for, we wouldn't actually like it! In my case, I need to embrace the waiting, keep praying for my future husband, writing to him on the nights of longing, and keep learning about becoming the woman of his prayers.

If anyone is reading this, when I'm long gone from this earth, know that today I'm praying for you in your "waiting rooms" too!

The notebook slides to the grass. "It's like she wrote it for someone to read, the way she worded it at the end." Shivers cover my body, prickling the tiny hairs on my arms and legs.

The sliding door opens, startling me. Cara calls out, saying they are going to bed.

"Coming," I tell her, gathering my things. There's no telling how long I would have been there, slightly dazed and awed at the relevance and impeccable timing of Grandma's words.

Great is Your faithfulness, God. Truly and honestly. I needed to hear her words and her passing away last year didn't stand in Your way of allowing me to do just that. Another thought. A curious feeling overtaking me. If I was getting insight and encouragement from my Grandma, who in the world would I be learning from next?

Only time would tell.

Chapter 5

Whether he has a six pack, muscular arms or is taller then you, won't matter when you are throwing up and need someone to hold your hair back and sooth you with love and kind words. Will the boy in question do this for you?

- **A quote I heard at church at a ladies banquet once and scribbled down on my bulletin.**

"What does that feel like?" Cara asks me, eyes wide. We are sitting on her couch, mid-afternoon on a Wednesday. She's still on maternity leave with Ruthie, otherwise she'd typically be in class, teaching cutie pie grade ones at Westberry Elementary School. Since they have another baby the way, it may be a while before she's back to full time teaching. As for my work, again it's raining. Since the shop is near spotless, the equipment all tuned up, the boss sent us home for the afternoon.

"On one hand, it's fascinating, with a touch of freaky." I hand Ruthie over to Cara, her hands now free to take the rosy cheeked and mused dark curls baby. The formula warmed, mixed with water and shaken, Cara places the bottle in Ruthie's mouth and cradles her. I've just confided in her what Emily knows about my future marriage. "But it's also annoying."

Cara adjusts Ruthie, so her head is propped up more. "How so?"

"Every time a guy comes across my path that interests me, at church or work, I find myself watching Emily's reaction."

A look of understanding. "Ah, to see if she approves."

"Yeah. And some of the guys at work are Christians and real Boaz types, from what I can tell so far. From things they say and do." I prop my feet up on the stool in front of me, starring at my rainbow smiley face socks. "But Emily looks disinterested when I talk about liking them. Sooo frustrating."

Cara is quiet. I appreciate getting to spend time with her. A nice surprise on the rainy days, with my sometimes sporadic schedule. She's not decades older than me but I think I can learn a lot from her. "I don't think you should base your decision to like someone solely off her facial expressions or lack of interest. She may just be trying to conceal her emotions, to not sway you, not realizing that her lack of emotions is making you think they aren't quality guys."

Emily did say that there are multiple wise choices out there. So it's not for me to necessarily find the one with the name she saw but allow God to help me chose a wise choice from the ones that come my way. Though if the name she saw was the best wise choice, I want to find him." Good point." Seeing Ruthie is done with her bottle, I open my arms. "Can I hold her?"

"Just let me burp her first, then she'll probably pass out on you." Cara holds the baby up against her chest, patting her back. "I believe she's telling you the truth, about knowing."

"You do?" It sounds so fantasy like and supernatural that I was hesitant to even say anything at first.

"Yes. Joey sometimes has characteristics of the Spiritual Gift of Knowledge. So I'm familiar with it." After a loud burp from Ruthie she passes her to me. I take the warm, sleepy baby and cradle her against myself. We lock eyes and Ruthie giggles, her chubby cheeks filling even more when she smiles. Eyes fluttering and tummy full of formula, she doesn't last long and gives into sleep. "And you said Emily sometimes texts you, saying she's praying for you, even when you haven't told her you're having a really bad day. Joey sometimes does that too." Cara stands and stretches her arms above her head. "May I suggest something?" When I nod, she pads into the kitchen and opens a draw. Finding a paper and pen, she comes back and sits down. "Write to him."

I stare at the page. "Seriously?"

"Dead serious."

After the spaghetti and meatballs, salad and corn on the cob have filled our tummies, the dishwasher loaded, my lunch for tomorrow made and sitting in the fridge in a paper bag, I sit down at my desk in my room.

And write.

Him.

Dear Future Husband,

Sometime I wonder where you are. Like right now. Are we in the same country? Town? Province? Have we met? I just don't know. And I suppose I don't need to know. I have to believe that God is still teaching us lessons separately, making us into the godly people we need each other to be. Sometimes I get sacred that I'll settle, since I can't find you in my timetable. I so desire to find a man who is passionately in love with Christ, who lights up talking about God, who talks about God more than himself, who finds such identity, fulfilment and security in his personal friendship with God and in living a Holy Spirit led life. The other day, when I brought these worries to God, He told me to trust Him and know He wouldn't disappoint me in the man He has planned for me. He will help me find a wise choice, even if it's not the one Emily saw.

I've been praying these last few days that you won't settle either. That you'll wait for me, wait for the godly woman God has and is transforming me into .The girl who stands out from culture's typical way of doing things and desires to do things God's way.

Oh! I could write pages and pages. But I don't know you yet, I don't know the love language you best respond to. I thrive by words of affirmation, written and verbal. But you may be a physical touch, quality time or acts of service love language man.

I just can't wait to meet you! To start a friendship and share laughter and countless conversations about God. How He's healed and changed and blessed us in our separate years. I want to be a power couple for The Kingdom of Christ, using our passions, talents and spiritual gifts, our testimonies and personal experiences to introduce people to Jesus. To increase faith in those who already have Him as a friend. I want your faith to be what turns my head and heart, to be a key or code word that ignites sparks, love and chemistry. I hope it's not years before we meet. Before our love story unfolds. But if so, God has a reason for the waiting. He doesn't make us wait to be cruel but so we can enjoy each other all the more, thanks to our single years forming us...

I set down my red pen and rub my eyes. The words seemed to flow. I'm not sure if this will be the first of many letters to come or the only one. But it felt good to write to him, to share my heart with him. I push back my chair and grab my pajamas from my dresser. I wash my face, brush my hair, change and am squirting my toothpaste on my toothbrush when I think of something else.

I can kind of communicate to him in another way, aside from writing letters on the lonely nights. I can pray. Maybe it's not like talking to him in person but I can still talk to God on his behalf. *And even if there are many wise choices out there, people that I could be compatible with for a godly, enjoyable marriage, God knows the one I'll marry. My prayers on his behalf will be appropriately directed.* I set down my toothbrush on the edge of the counter and grip both sides of the sink. Slowly, I lift my eyes to meet my reflection's wide-eyes. It dawns on me that right now, my future spouse is living and breathing somewhere in this world. In this town? Back in Saskatoon? Maybe in a different country? I don't know. But somewhere he is walking and living life with people at school, home and work, just like me. I picture a faceless guy waking up in the mornings, getting reading, going to school or work, coming home. He must experience hardships and temptations and discouragement, like us all.

I can help protect him and lift him up, through prayer. The Bible says in James the prayers of a God loving person can accomplish much. Knowing that, I vow to prayer for this nameless boy often, to pray for him things I would like prayed for me in this season of my life.

A prayer warrior even before we meet.

***

The rest of the week flies by. The days are full of working outdoors in my hot beige canvas overalls, sometimes with Emily and Brandon, sometimes not, mowing schoolyards, weed whacking fence lines, watering flowers in parks and the hanging pots down Main Street. That's actually my favorite job, being given the keys to the watering truck for the day. Yes, I'm on my own all day, aside from breaks, but I just pop in my ear buds and water the day away.

Sunday morning is the first day of June. It's sunny, a blue sky full of puffy white clouds. I wake earlier then my alarm, pull on some dark skinny jeans, a flowery dress shirt and a grey affinity scarf. After braiding my hair into a single French braid down my back, I join the rest of the family at the breakfast table.

"I think I'm going to practice special music once more before I get Grandpa." I sit down next to Joey at the table.

Cara fills a glass of orange juice for me and sets it in front of me. She gestures to the oven. "There are waffles in there and scrambled eggs on the stove." Taking her finished plate to the sink, she comes back with some baby food for Ruthie.

I make a goofy face at the baby. Sitting in her high chair, she wears a grey bib with a blue whale on it. The words, "I whaley like you, Mommy" are written underneath the image of the whale. Ruthie claps her hands, a new skill learned, and squeals loudly when I make a monkey face.

"Feeling nervous?" Joey mops up the last of his maple syrup with his cut up waffle.

Plucking a green grape from the bowl near me, I stand and nod. Forgetting yet again he can't see, I chide myself. "A bit but once I start playing it will be okay. I've loved that song since the first time Grandma April sang it to me instead of a bed time book." Standing, I head to the stove to fix myself a plate of the divinely smelling breakfast. Ruthie's breakfast doesn't look so good. Smashed peas and cheerios are no comparison to waffles. "Sometime I feel bad for Ruthie, having to watch us eat all this amazing food." I sit back down a few minutes later, scooting my chair closer to the table.

Joey reaches over to ruffle his daughter's dark hair. "The wait will be worth it. If she started eating things before her system could handle it, it wouldn't be good for her."

Thirty minutes later, I'm sitting in a grassy area near Caleb. I have Jack's guitar with me. As I play, I savor the feel of the sun on my skin and the sight of the golden tall fields in the distance, the soft green grass underneath me, and the evergreens surrounding me.

Waiting for my guy is like Ruthie waiting to be introduced to more solids. If they let her eat too many new things, they'd never know what she was allergic to, if she reacted. And her little tummy wouldn't feel good. What if I met the boy with the name Emily saw today? Maybe I wouldn't even be attractive to him. Maybe since he isn't the person I need him to be yet, a reason why we haven't met yet, maybe he would even annoy me today! And vice versa.

"Great is Thy Faithfulness..." I softly sing the lyrics as I play my guitar. Before I know it, I'm picking it up again, this time exchanging my grass stage for a real one.

"This is a song my grandma used to always sing," I tell the audience, putting the strap of my guitar over my head. "The lyrics are timeless and I love how they speak life to me." Positioning me closer to the mike, I pay a few intro chords then dive into the famous hymn. Throughout the next four minutes, I play a combination of G, C, D, E and A minors as I sing. I build my voice during the chorus parts, embracing my unique soulful sound.

One line stands out as I sing. "Summer and winter, spring time and harvest…" The naming of the seasons and the ending of the verse saying, "To thy great faithfulness, mercy and love," reminds me that just as God has been faithful to me before, providing great friendships in the fall and a good job near family in spring and summer, so He will continue to be faithful in the approaching months and seasons.

When the last line has been sung, I do a little curtesy. Removing my guitar strap, I set it near the back of the stage then return to my seat. Emily, hair prettily curled for church, gives me a thumbs up from a few rows over and Brandon winks.

The sermon that day comes and goes, a guest speaker who served as a missionary in Rwanda taking the pulpit for forty minutes. After saying hello to some of the congregation, including my friends, I leave with Grandpa to walk back to Caleb. Cara, Ruthie and Joey are going to meet us there.

"What's for lunch?" I ask Grandpa as we walk the paved path to Caleb.

"The menu posted in the elevator said roast beef and the fixings," he says, slowly walking with the assistance of a cane. Each day the cook post the menu inside the elevator for residents to see. Typically their larger meal is the noon meal, with supper being more of a sandwich and soup affair.

When we enter Caleb, a large and fancy looking building, similar to a four floor hotel, Grandpa waves to the receptionist. His eyes twinkle, his wrinkles growing more noticeable when he smiles. "That sweetheart has a sweet tooth. I always make sure to give her a peppermint."

I laugh as I follow him into the dining room. The room is decorated to have the feel of home. There are soft green walls and pictures of the residents doing outings and playing cards hang on the wall. Multiple round tables with white table clothes and comfy looking chairs fill the room. Large windows allow for light to warm and brighten the moods of residents.

"Everyone, this is my granddaughter, Lyndzi," my grandpa says, stopping beside a table full of seniors." She and a few others are joining us for lunch today."

"Hello, everyone," I wave, sliding into an empty seat next to Grandpa. I observe my lunch mates, who have become close friends to my grandpa. There are a few woman but more men. I assume one man and woman are a couple since they are holding hands on top of the table. I'm the only one without white hair or who's wearing less than one layer of clothing, despite the sunny weather outside and the warm temperature of the dining room. They are adorable though, the women with their permed white curls and clip on earrings and the men with their old fashioned train conductor hats, sweater vests and ironed slacks. If I were to peer underneath the table, I bet many of them would be wearing slippers. I politely chat with them, telling them about wanting to become a nurse and that I'm staying with Cara and Joey for the summer.

"Did someone say my name?"

I look up to find Joey approaching the table, diaper bag hanging off his shoulder. He removes his aviator sunglasses. Though he's legally blind, he can still detect light. Some people use it to orient themselves but he told me he finds it more of a nuisance, especially when playing piano. Cara and I sometimes have to remind him to remove his sunglasses when he gets indoors.

Cara sits next to me, Ruthie on her lap. The baby looks content, for now. She may want to crawl around and explore once the novelty of stationary observing new surroundings and faces wear off. A worker comes by with a highchair and my curly haired cousin smiles her thanks. After putting the baby in the seat, Cara turns to me. "I had forgotten how beautiful your voice is, Lyndzi."

Grandpa pats my knee. "Takes after her grandma. Sings like an angel." He turns to address his friends. "Lyndzi sang a wonderful version of my April's favorite hymn this morning in church." The servers bring by our plates of food then. Already plated, the meal consist of steamed green beans, roast beef, garlic mashed plates with gravy, and cheese and chive biscuits with butter.

For the most part, Ruthie is the topic of our conversation. Her giggles and toothy grins gain the attention of the woman. They "ooh" and "ahh" over her, smiles stretching wide when Cara offers to let them hold her after Ruthie's eaten her banana wafers and mashed berries.

I stare at the couple holding hands. Ernest and Betty, I think their names were. They keep sharing secret smiles. The love in their eyes is heart melting. *I want that so bad someday.* "Do you have any relationship advice," I suddenly ask, surprising myself.

Betty sets down her fork and wipes her mouth with her burgundy cloth napkin. Setting it back on her lap, she leans closer to me across the table. "Be prepared to forgive him lots and to be forgiven lots by him."

Edward Frank directs his gaze to me, wrinkled face serious. He's one of the ones wearing an old fashioned train conductor hat. "Make sure you know the fellow enough to know you can trust and depend on him." I nod, thoughtful and appreciative of his advice.

To Edward Frank's right, Martha Jean adjusts her glasses, the kind that have a chain to hang them around your neck. "And don't forget the 80% rule."

"What's that?" Grandpa asks, reaching for a peppermint in his pocket. He hands them out as Martha Jean explains.

"Some days you'll only be able to give 80% of yourself to your spouse. You might be sick or overwhelmed. Some say marriage is a 50/ 50 deal." She shakes her white head of hair, the sparkly turquoise clip on the side of her white curls catching the light. "Not true. On the drained days, your spouse may need to give his 100% plus the 20% you can't."

Ernest speaks up, looking away from his wife. "Some days you will be the one giving extra and some days you will be the one receiving it. But don't keep score."

I make designs with my fork with the leftover gravy on my plate. "Interesting."

"Selfless love is what marriage is all about, Lyndzi," Cara says, standing to take Ruthie from one of the men who needed to leave to find a restroom. "One of the hardest parts of marriage, since thinking of someone else isn't something we naturally do."

It isn't until after a dessert of pecan brownies and ice-cream and another hour of conversation that I bring up the topic again. We are walking back to the house now, stomachs full and hearts content from the good conversation. "But isn't that impossible? To love and care for someone more than 100%?"

Joey holds the door open and Cara slips past to put Ruthie down for her afternoon nap. He gestures to the step and I sit down next to him. "Absolutely impossible on your own." He gazes out across the street at the church, his home away from home, not really seeing it. But maybe picturing it how it looked before his accident at twenty. "But with God, you can tap into a supernatural love."

We are quiet, both lost in our own wolds and memories.

"Joey?" I finally ask, breaking the silence. "Do you think God wants me to be single right now?"

"Yes, I do. Just from watching you these last few weeks, He's clearly teaching you a lot, preparing you for marriage." He rolls up the sleeves of his white dress shirt and then leans back against his elbows, long legs stretched out. "I know God doesn't call everyone to marriage but I think He has you."

I get shivers, remembering Cara saying Joey sometimes knows things like Emily does.

"Your countdown clock is on. Your single years limited. Use this unique time to love God and others, distraction free." Unlooping his red tie from around the neck of his white dress shirt, he sets it beside him. His blue eyes find mine. Even though he's handsome, I know Cara found a man even more attractive on the inside. I hope to find a "Joey" of my own someday. "Tell me one thing, Lyndzi."

I unlatch the buckle of my brown gladiator sandals, slip them off, and then hug my knees to my chest. “Sure.”

“Would you rather be single and living life joyfully and to the fullest for God, or be married and miserable?”

That’s easy. “The first scenario.” It clicks suddenly, what Joey is trying to tell me. “Marriage doesn’t necessarily make you any happier.”

“Nope. It’s a lot of work, daily, and its two people bringing their own flaws, weakness and struggles into close proximity. Sometimes two unhappy singles become one unhappy couple.”

Hearing a cry from inside, Joey stands. “I better go see if Cara needs help.” I remain where I am, a lot of thinking and processing ahead of me. The door creaks open but I don’t hear it close. I turn to find Joey looking down at me, meeting my eyes straight on as he occasionally does. “He’s going to be worth the wait, Lyndzi. Don’t settle, he’s out there. You’re not the only one waiting.” What he says next causes my stomach to flutter, my hopes for the future soar. “And from the transformation God is doing on you, in this waiting season, it’s clear you’re going to be worth waiting for too.”

***

“Do you like being pregnant?”

Cara shrugs, massaging her seven month pregnant belly. “When I’m not nauseous or thinking about the pain of delivery.” Her voice grows quiet. “Or thinking about the baby weight I’ve gained.”

It's Thursday, early evening. Grandpa was going to visit his old friends in Kerrobert this week so we are cat-sitting Cali. Ruthie and Joey are out in the backyard, playing on a new baby swing set. From the shrieks of baby delight and adult laugher coming through the open window, I can easily picture the two of them wearing their identical contagious grins. "I used to say I didn't want biological children," Cara confess. We're sitting at the table, our Uno game forgotten. "I was insecure as it was, in a thin body. How would I handle a curvier and heavier pregnant body?"

I pat my knee and Cali hops up onto my lap. She quickly settles down, wrapping her tail around herself as she lays down. I stroke her soft fur, glad to spend a few extra days in her company. She's been sleeping with me at night, curled up at the foot of the bed, like she does usually at Grandpa's. "What changed?" I'm aware of Cara's past struggle with an eating disorder. I've heard her speak on how God used counselling and later Joey, to help her to heal. To show her to look at her body as individual limbs, powerful to listen, lift up or walk alongside hurting people who need Jesus.

She fingers a red Uno card. Cara's hair is short now, curling even more wildly. Ruthie's strong yanks of her longer locks caused her to book an appointment last week. I think my cousin looks beautiful either way. "A conversation Joey and I had, a few weeks after we were married." She closes her eyes and as she paints out the long ago scene of a yesterday gone by, I feel like I'm there myself...

"Hey, what cha doing?" Joey asks Cara, sitting down at the piano bench at the church. It's a familiar spot for them, one they spent many evenings and afternoons giggling and falling in love on.

Cara plays a scale, trailing her fingers over the black and white keys. "About the future." From the tone of her voice, Joey knows there's something serious on her heart. He finds her hands and places his own on top of them, stopping her from playing. She sighs, then leans into his chest. "I'm scared of getting pregnant. I'm just starting to accept this body."

Joey strokes her blond curls, knowing her pain is real, realizing the mental scars of anorexia will never be completely gone. "We don't have to have biological kids, Cara. We can always adopt." He gently eases her back and lifts her chin up with hand, forcing her to meet his eyes. "But I think being afraid shows your disorder still controls you a bit."

A shudder. A tear falling. Symbolizing the ach within, the war and struggle of wants and abilities. "I know having a baby is so worth a changing body but I'm scared."

Again Joey pulls her close. "I know. But what if we walked the process together? And marvelled at what the changes in your body were creating? What our love created?"

After wiping her eyes on the shoulder of her white and black striped long sleeve, Cara sniffs. "It would be amazing to know we created another human being together, because of loving each other."

"It's amazing what love can do."

Cara's voice trails off as the memory finishes. Gathering my bearings, the image of the church auditorium fades and the kitchen comes back to view. I study Cara. "So when the right man came along, you were able to conquer your fear?"

"Yes, I realized after our conversation at the piano that I actually *wanted* to create a baby with him. To have parts of our individual personalities and appearances create a unique individual. Another member of our family." She starts to gather the yellow, red, green and blue cards before us. "1 John 4:18 says 'Perfect love casts out fear."

I help her with the cards. "So God and Joey helped you."

"Exactly. God alone allows Joey to love me supernaturally."

We share a smile. "The 80% rule," we say in union and chuckle.

"Make no mistake," Cara says, placing the stack of cards back into the box. "I still have days when I look at a past photo of me, pre-pregnancy days, and moan. Or when I pull on my maternity swimsuit or look at my swollen and stretched stomach when I'm getting dressed." She shakes her head, obviously not wanting to go down that lane long. "But Joey still kisses me every morning before he goes to work, saying I'm more beautiful to him then the day before." She looks down at her bump, smiling. "And being around Ruthie all day, although she's unquestionably exhausting, even more so now that she's crawling all over the place, she reminds me it's all worth it in the end." In perfect timing, happy child laughter filters in the window.

A few minutes later, Joey and Ruthie appear, giggling and smiling up a storm. I watch the little family interact and use the longing in my heart as a reminder to pray. For the man that God will someday send my way, when the time is right and my relationship tool box has all I need.

***

"You guys have never kissed?" I can't believe I'm hearing Emily correct. "Haven't you been seriously dating, like, for over half a year?"

Brandon looks back at me, sitting in the backseat. "She won't let my lips near her face." He receives a one handed shove from Emily in the driver's seat. We're carpooling back to Saskatoon this weekend. For a mud run called Dirty Donkey, at Blackstrap Provincial Park. "Kidding!" he says, rubbing the spot where she hit him.

"But why?"

Emily catches my eye in the rear-view mirror. "I told him on date number two that I have some standards. If he wanted to be my guy, he had better memorize them, respect them and comply with them."

Again Brandon turns. His blond hair is covered with a navy beanie. "Emily told me, over our delectable dessert at Moxie's of their deadly white chocolate brownie, that she wouldn't hold my hand, kiss me, or be kissed by me, dance with me, hug me or, watch a movie in the dark, aside from at the theatres, or be alone at my house after eleven."

"Ever?" I realize my mouth is unattractively hanging open and close it.

"Not until we get married," Emily answers. "These standards might seem pretty old fashioned to you but I want to save everything to experience with my husband. So nothing we do brings up memories of having done it with others. It's my gift to him and in the end I benefit too. No comparing, no remembering unwanted memories."

Hmm, intriguing. Maybe not for everything, to be so extreme but it definitely has appealing benefits, of giving such a beautiful gift to your future husband.

The remainder of our two hour drive back to the city is full of laughter and fun conversation. Our wave of runners is set to go at ten-thirty tomorrow morning. Once in the city, we grab some food at Center Mall food court, take in a movie, buy some candy at the store near the mall cinema and then go eat it in the park behind myself. Around midnight we part and head to our separate houses. We're all keeping our apartments for the summer, paying rent still, but then enjoying not having to store, move our things or find a new place for the fall.

"Morning, sunshine!" Emily tells me when I slip into her parked car around eight-forty-five the next morning.

"How many cups of coffee has she had?" I mumble at Brandon as I put my seatbelt on in the back.

He passes me a takeout cup from Tim Horton's. "Two that I was there to witness."

Blackstrap is thirty minutes from Saskatoon. Because of the early hour and our late bedtime last night, we are all pretty subdued. Even Emily, once her coffee kick wears off.

Handing the parking attendant our newly purchased provincial park pass, we drive up through the steep roads. Then find a place to park next to the many other cars parked on the grass. After signing in with a woman in a tent near the start line, we take off our layers and pin our white race bibs to our fronts. Pulling on knee length green socks, red clown noses and tie-dyed afro wigs, we snap a few group shots, pre-mud run.

We ran this same race the year before. Just in boring shorts and t-shirts though. After watching so many teams come in crazy team outfits, we decided to do the same this year.

“Remember last year when you took your pony tail out?” Emily asks, grinning at the memory as she stretches her calf.

“It stayed in perfect pony tale potion without the elastic in.” It was amusing yet disturbing how much mud had been in my hair. Took multiple lathers of shampoo to get it all out.

Beside me, Brandon is jumping in place, trying to stay warm. “The worst part is the drive home.”

“True that.” Typically they run out of water for the later heat times that finished the 5km obstacle run. The water truck can only hold so much. Last year we ended up just leaving without hosing off, sitting on towels in our car. From the shocked sounds coming from the water truck, the water had been freezing anyways. Wiping ourselves off with towels hadn’t been that bad.

I check my watch and tell them we should head over to the start gate. We walk by food tents, multiple groups of other costumed clad teams, the sign in place and a pile of muddy shoes. “I think it’s awesome that they clean up the shoes and donate them,” I say, knowing I’ll do the same again this year. “Last year I tried to wash my clothes but ended up filing my washer with dirt, mud and grass.” This year I planned to just toss my clothes afterwards. Not worth the mess of cleaning.

We freeze as we wait for our heat to be announced. We jump in place, we do jumping jacks. We stretch and complain about the cold. We laugh. We chat with other teams Then the race director appears, gives us a few instructions, shoots his gun and we are off!

Through mud pits we jump, up an old ski hill we run. We pull ourselves with a rope through a waist deep swamp. Down a huge slip and slide we tumble down. Over climbing walls we boast each up. Through blue dumpsters with mud we wade. We pull heavy objects together as a team and run many kilometres in between each obstacle, panting, and faces smeared with mud, laughing and loving the challenge and feeling of being warriors being chased through a jungle. An hour of pure fun and hard work, both individually and as a team.

The last obstacle is my favorite: climbing over a parked semi.

“I feel so beastly,” I grunt, placing a mud caked hand on the first rung of the rope latter swung against the semi.

“You look like one,” Emily says, looking down at me.

“Both ya smell like one too!” Brandon says from the top, waving. His afro wig is comically full of mud and grass. Emily looks about the same and I assume I make three. We may have started out in bright colors but we are all brown now. And my pants were capris at the start line but from all the mud weighing them down, it’s like I have full length pants on now.

My team waits for me at the top of the semi. On the count of three, we jump down together into the mud pit. We swim through the mud, getting it on our teeth, in our eyes and in our mouths.

I spit out a mouthful when we climb out of the mud river. One eye is full of mud. Brandon splashed me by accidently as he breast stroked by me. I wipe at my eye without success. There is no clean part of me to use!

Shrugging, I keep my eye clamped shut and run after my team. One by one we hoot and holler as we jump through the ring of fire finish line.

"Yeah ya, baby!" Brandon shouts ahead of me. "I'm on fi-ya!"

I sprinted the last part my hardest, how I always like to finish when run. Bending, I try to catch my breath. "That was awesome."

"There were some new obstacles this year," Emily says, handing me a chocolate milk and a purple bandanna with the mud run logo on it. Our complimentary gifts post-race. "The fire's a new one."

"I am the man!" Brandon yells, beating his chest. People chuckle around us and Emily and I roll our eyes.

We drink our chocolate milk, get some pictures with fun poses, decide to get hosed down, donate our shoes and then go back to the car.

I'm quiet on the way back to Saskatoon. Yes, I'm looking forward to a long hot shower but something more. Just as the mud run was hard but fun, so will be a future relationship. I'm looking forward to the starting line of it. The nerves, the excitement, the learning curve. I hadn't known what to expect last year when I ran Dirty Donkey but this year I was more prepared. But I equally enjoyed each year's mud run. Surprises can be good things. *Like the timing of meeting a certain someone.*

Once I'm home, after having mud pooling at my ankles in a long shower, comfy sweats and an old t-shirt in place, I stretch in my living room.

And smile.

Big.

I'll make a better girlfriend now then I would've at the beginning of the week. God's placing some wise people, life analogies, and educational conversations in my path lately. Cara, Joey, Grandpa, Grandma's journals, Emily and Brandon, even those adorable residents at Caleb.

I tug at my hamstring and grin, even though the stretch slightly hurts.

Just think of what I'll have learned by the time it's time to go back to Saskatoon for school. And if I'm learning so much, he must be too. Can't wait to compare one day, what we were both doing on this very day…

Chapter 6

"Just because he is a Boaz, doesn't mean he's *your* Boaz."

- **From a book Emily loaned me, called "A Man worth waiting for" by Jackie Kendal**

Ben Johnson, 28 years old, long-term resident of Kindersley:

It's Sunday, June 16th, the day of the long anticipated mud run. My buddies and I, all volunteers from the Kindersley Fire Department, signed up for the extreme 10 km version. Some of the guys had run the race the previous year, not me.

"The 10km didn't really have any more obstacle then the 5km last year," Greg comments, turning right onto the highway from the gravel road. Even from the backseat, I can see mud intertwined with his dirty blond hair. Our heat finished fifteen minutes ago. The game plan is to drive back to Stoon and grab some food. Votes around were anonymous for a breakfast place. Maybe Grainfields or Cora's.

Yeah, I feel kind of disgusting, with dried mud packed on myself, despite having rinsed off with the giant hose and rubbed off with my towel. But whatever, a delayed shower with feel all the better. *And I'd rather fill my stomach first. Lord knows, Greg won't have anything other than peanut butter and pop tarts in his cupboards.* Most of us live in Kindersley but Greg's only home for the summer. He's in his second year of law at the U of S. We're all crashing at his condo in the city this weekend. His roommates are gone for the summer too, so we have the place to our self.

"Yeah, I thought there would be more obstacles or at least more extreme ones," Elliot comments, chugging his fourth chocolate milk carton. They were handing them out in the food tent area. "The 10 km just had more distance in-between them. When I was waiting to buy my perogies and sausage at the food truck, the girl behind me described the 5km obstacles. Most of them were the same as ours."

My stomach lurches. How Elliot could have ate perogies and sausage pre-race and then got another plate after is beyond me. A human tank, for sure. A stomach of steel? *Oh, yeah*. Running is my preferred form of exercise. Usually without music or company. It's my solitude, a time and place to think and pray. What have I been praying about lately? Mostly *her.*

"Hey, Ben!"

I jerk from my thoughts, pulling my gaze from the window of passing prairie scenes. The skies overcast today and lighting and rain had begun just as our team was near the fire loop finish line. "Yeah?"

Martin, with his blond hair longer than any of us guys, wearing his typical backwards Rough Rider football hat, is giving me a weird look. "Where's your head at, man?"

I start to run my hands through my dark hair then stop. I feel dried mud and don't want to get Greg's precious "baby" dirty. His 1974 Rider green mustang, with black vertical stripes down the hood is his pride and joy. "Sorry, I was just thinking."

"Seriously, man. I'm talking about those babes! You missed out. They had psychedelic colored afro wigs on. And those legs? Even in them long socks, I was loving the beautiful view!" Martin punches me in the shoulder and I grunt. He's the linebacker on our fireman football team, The Hotshots. The guy's massive, easily closer to three hundred pounds then two-fifty. Elliot ate seconds of the greasy food from the race. But Martin? I think he had fifths. At all the organized runs I've done, half marathons, or 10kms, it always surprises me that they offer unhealthy food. *Though the Bridge City Boogie had oranges and water last week,* I think, recalling the Saskatoon family run I did with my nineteen year old brother, Andrew.

The guys have moved onto a new topic, not dwelling on my quietness. Aside from Greg, they aren't Christians but that doesn't make me love them less. But I see it as a God given opportunity to show them how a person living for God's will lives different. Sometimes I get quiet, usually when I'm praying, and they just move on, talking shop about girls, sports, work or food. The main themes of our conversations.

"Show them that we care about them and their stories first," Greg told me once when it was just him and I on an overnight shift at the fire hall. "Then they'll care about hearing about our testimony and about the story of God's healing touch."

I'd nodded, leaning against the counter as I microwaved a frozen lasagna in the break room. "Form a relationship with them, then an interest in a relationship with Christ may follow."

"There's something different about you two," Martin mentioned once. He and I were polishing the front of the fire truck one rainy afternoon. "But in a good way." It was the best compliment ever. Reminding me that the small can be significant. That those around me in the workplace are watching and observing, like researchers. How do Greg and

Ben handle disappointment, do they get angry? How do they treat woman? Do they use crude or dirty language?

My thoughts sift to my sermon notes from a few Sundays ago.

-Men are created to be the leaders, don't take that away from them. Let him pursue you, women. There should be no question if he is interested. You are worth being pursued properly, in person, not mainly over social media. Like he is a dying man in the desert and you are water.

- Men, a woman should make your man feel ten feet tall, respected and needed.

It's a topic that Pastor Joey spoke on during one sermon this summer. Usually I attend a different church, the same as my parent's, my roommate and Greg. But I slept in that morning. So I attended the eleven o'clock service at Pastor Joey's church, instead of the ten-fifteen one at my regular one. *But I think God wanted me to be there that Sunday. Reminds me of that poem, the one where the guy is angry at God for not helping him get to work on time. He yells that God could have delayed the train. Then God says, kindly and patiently, something about placing the train there so the man would miss the van going through a red light.*

I see the outskirts of Saskatoon come into view. Beside me, Martin's stomach growls. "Seriously?" I ask. "Didn't you just feed that thing?"

He shrugs his large shoulders. "It's a bottomless pit, can't stay full. Guess all the days of my life I'm gonna be chomping." A big belly laugh escapes, his stomach jiggling. "But I ain't complaining! My momma taught this big boy to clean his plate real good!"

I laugh. Martin's awesome. And I really appreciate how his sense of humor is clean and he makes an effort to not curse around me or Greg.

All the days of life... why does that sound so familiar? It's not until we pull up to Cora's, a speciality breakfast chain that gives you fruit in decorative displays that my thoughts fully form.

"All the days of her life, she brings honour to her husband." That's the verse Martin's words triggered. It's in proverbs, talking about a woman. But after the waitress in a purple polo shirt leads us to our corner table, hands us our menus, and takes our drink orders, something clicks.

You could totally switch the pronouns in that verse, to apply it to a male perspective. When the waitress returns, I order a stack of chocolate chip crepes and a side of fruit, three scrambled eggs and bacon. I'm contributing to the conversation but I'm not wholeheartedly in it.

All the days of his life, all the days of his life.... I can't stop repeating that phrase. *That includes honoring her with my life style choices, how I interact with woman and the neglected, even before we meet. All the days of my life includes prior to God crossing our paths.*

"You're quiet," Greg says later, washing his hands beside me. The others are paying. He and I both headed to the bathroom after we paid.

"Just thinking."

"About her." It isn't a question. He knows what's been on my mind lately. We were best friends in high school and even though he moved for school, we're still close as brothers.

I lean against the sink, away from a reflection of a mud streaked, brown haired guy. My last girlfriend said I was her dream guy come to life, with my, and I quote, '"Tall, enviably tanned even in winter, and handsome face." But honestly, I think I'm just average. And I sometimes get mistaken for another person. *Incredibly awkward when someone throws their arms around you or runs giddily up to you and you have to tell them that no, I don't recognize you, nor have we ever met.* "Yeah. Maria and I have been broken up for three years and I haven't gone on one date yet."

Greg yanks some paper towel off from the automatic dispense then balls it up before tossing it in the trash. A hand to my shoulder. "Keep praying for her, man. She's out there. Most likely she's wondering where you are too, needing prayer for patience too."

I open my mouth to ask if "What if maybe God's prefect will and plan for my life doesn't include a wife?" but Greg shakes his head, one step ahead of me. "No prayers go to waste. You're still drawing closer to God through them, even if the woman of your prayers never appears." I nod and we start to leave but then he suddenly stops, hand positioned to push open the swinging door into the noisy restaurant. "And Ben?"

"Yeah?"

"At the end of your life, you're never going to regret surrendering to God's will. You won't be saying, 'I wish I had settled and not waited for a wise choice of a woman to come along. I wish I hadn't waited for someone who shares my love of Jesus, who has a compatible life calling, life style, finance and family direction."

My muscles ache from sitting so long without proper stretching. I tiredly rub my face, some dried mud crumbling off. "Our joy is only as satisfying as our surrender is real," I quote him, referring to something he texted me during those painful initial days post breakup from a two year relationship with Maria. Greg was telling me then the same thing he is today. There is no joy outside of God's will. Not lasting, at least. His will isn't always the easiest, ahem like this waiting and longing period, but it's the most satisfying and life giving in the end.

A small smile from my buddy. "Exactly. Solid relationships aren't found, Ben. They are formed. You could create a satisfying and passionate godly relationship with numerous woman." A frown. "Well, but only with one. But it could work with numerous options. So don't put too much pressure on yourself to find The One."

A snort. "Gotcha."

And as I follow him back into the restaurant, I know God knows. The future is laid out crystal clear to him. All I have to do is read the first nine words of the famous Jeremiah 29:11 Bible verse. He knows if I'll marry. He knows what girl to direct my prayers to for my future wife, who they belong to, if she exists.

And that, gives me peace of mind, at least for now.

***

Lyndzi:

"You are ..." Emily sits back on her hind legs, searching for the right adjective. "Weird? Unique? Adorable?" She bends back down, scooping some of the freshly laid down top soil to make a small hole. Today we were paired together at work, to plant bedding flowers around town. Right now were at the pool, sitting in their square flower bed. It's

Tuesday, our first day back from the long weekend and the mud run.

I brush off dirt from the knees of my overalls and stand. Taking off my work gloves, I wipe a hand across my sweaty forehead. *It's so hot in these things, especially in our plus 29 Celsius weather today.* I wish we didn't have to wear such heavy overalls. But it's company policy. "Taking selfies with Cali is cool," I defend myself, stepping out of the garden box to grab more black plastic crates of red petunias. Flowers in hand, I sit back down next to her. But instead of helping, I cross my legs and start drawing circles in the dirt with a stick. "Besides, I only have so many weeks left to spend with her. I want to make the memories last. Pictures do just that."

Emily looks up from digging with a small shovel. There is dirt above her eyebrow. I don't tell her. I think it's funnier when she's unaware. At lunch I'll thoroughly enjoy Brandon telling her, in some comedic way. "Make sure to give your Grandpa some shots of that. He'll love that."

I press the release button on my red contigo water bottle, opening the top and take a long chug. Wiping my face with my sleeve, I smile. "After Cali and I came in from playing outside, Grandpa asked what we were doing." I resume my planting, feeling bad watching Emily plant rows of yellow marigolds. I squeeze a red petunia from the carton, freeing the stringy white roots from the bottom of the plastic package. "What the heck is a selfi?" I say, mimicking my grandpa's voice as best as I can.

Emily smiles.

I dig a hole and set the flower inside, covering it with dirt and then patting around the area. We'll water the flower bed real good before we leave. "He was like, 'Why do you call it a selfie if there are two of you are in it?"

"He has a good point. I never thought of that." A look of concentration. "Maybe it doesn't count if there are two..."

We switch spots, so I can place some red flowers amongst her marigolds. "Anyways, I ended up staying there another hour, taking selfies with Grandpa on the couch in his room."

Emily's face lights up. "Aww! That's so cute, Lyndzi!" When the final flower is planted for this section, we survey our hard work. "A beauty." Emily comments, nodding her head.

"The best."

Emily rises to her feet, gathering the opened bags of top soil and miracle growth, small shovels and the empty black plastic containers. She places them on the ground in one big pile. I could gather the hose up and wind it up but there's something that's been gnawing at me. For a while. Now seems like a good time to bring it up.

"Hey, Em, I need to ask you something kinda deep."

She doesn't look up from bending to pick up an unused plastic bag of soil. "Shoot," she grunts. Those things are heavy. I stand, helping her take it to the truck parked on the lawn a few feet away. We heave it into the back and then return to the flower bed to get the rest of our stuff.

"What was the point of God telling you I would get married someday? "At this she makes eye contact. Her eyes are understanding, as if she's been expecting this question for some time. "To reassure me? That I'll get married someday? Or so you can pray for specific things for me during this marriage preparation and season of waiting?" Once I've started, I can't stop. "Or why did He tell you a name? I don't see the benefit of that. But I fully believe that God doesn't do things like that for no reason." I kick at a stray container that Emily missed. "I just don't get it, Em. I really don't."

Slowly she bends and picks the kicked container. Rising, she tosses it from hand to hand. She's not looking at me, not because she's nervous but because she's concentrating. Finally she lifts her dark head, vibrant blue eyes full of compassion for my confusion." I think God is kind and sometimes give us reassurances in human form. Lyndzi, you desire to live for God and I know you pray for your dreams to match His plans for your life. And you are learning to be content and satisfied with God, not in a marriage." A long sigh. "Everyone has a Jesus shaped hole in their heart. Only once you find purpose, identity and satisfaction in God and loving others, can you healthy participate in a godly relationship? Don't be God to each other. He might be a great guy but he'll most definitely be a lousy god."

I recognize the "Jesus shaped hole" imagery she's using. It's from the book, "Love Without limits" by Nick Vujcic, currently on my bedside table. It's a book about a Christian man born without arms or legs who found meaning and purpose through God and his unique situation. He doesn't find his wife until nearly thirty. *I like how he got married later in life. Sometimes I feel like my parents and everyone just expects me to get married in my early young adult years. But there's nothing wrong with me if I don't.*

Emily reaches for my gloved hand and squeezes. "God told me I could tell you because He wanted to ease your worries that marriage wouldn't happen. It's a gift of reassurance that not everyone gets, girl. He never said when though, so the wait could be long." She sets the container down and then pulls me into a hug. "But oh-so worth it, friend. Just wait for God's leading and timing and that man of you prayers will appear. Wonderful yet flawed and loved by Christ, just as you are." She didn't answer all my questions but that's okay. We probably would've stay in our hug longer if I hadn't smelt something.

Burning.

"Do you smell that?" I ask, pulling apart, sniffing the air.

Emily breaths in deep, eyes widening with alarm. "Yeah, I do. Where's it coming from?"

I open my mouth to say I'm not sure when suddenly I see flames.

About four hundred meters from us.

I gasp.

I point.

Emily turns and echoes my horrified expression.

The rink located beside the pool is on fire. Angry licks of red and orange color roar at the top of the building. Massive black clouds of smoke cascade above the Quonset shaped white and brown rink. Within seconds we hear the fire siren, indicating that the volunteer firefights should report to the fire hall. I picture the town abuzz, phones beeping and vibrating with texts, heads looking up from desks and from browsing grocery aisle, hearing the fire sirens, worry and curiosity filling faces and minds.

"Grandpa!" I shout, suddenly my fear over spilling from deep within. I yank Emily towards me, my eyes wide. "Cara dropped him off for bingo today, at the rink!"

"Lyndiz, no!" This time she shakes me. "Brandon's grandma goes to that. It doesn't start until noon." She points to her cheap plastic white watch. "It's only ten-forty-five."

I don't have time to explain. I run back to the truck and hop in. She'll find a ride back to the shop. This is more important. My next four words I call out, backing the white work truck up, will have to satisfy her for now:

"He always goes early."

Chapter 7

Can you be yourself with them comfortably? Unapologetically? Can you be silly and also have those serious moments?

- **A line from a poem I wrote in my journal recently.**

The next two hours of my life are a blur of insanity. I'm in a constant state of panic, anxiety and rushing. "What if's?" plague me, hounding me like a pack of savage wolves. They nip at my mind, grazing as they please.

"God, please protect Grandpa," I plead, as I try to reach Cara or Joey. As suspected, phone lines are jammed. Everyone's texting or calling, trying to make sure loved ones are safe. I'm on my way to Caleb, hoping to find Grandpa napping, having missed his ride to the rink.

I spot a flash of white.

I swerve the car over.

"Cali!" I open the truck door. "Here, kitty, kitty!"

She looks up from licking her paw. I swear she smiles. She strolls across the street, not bothering to look if it's safe. "Meow!" she says, sitting on her hind legs in front of the opened door, cocking her head to one side.

"Naughty, kitty," I say swiftly picking her up her and bringing her into the truck. Shutting the door, I look over at her, already curled up in the passenger seat. "How did you get out, Cali?" Usually she's content staying inside or sleeping on Grandpa's fourth floor balcony. Or when I take her to play with Ruthie in Cara and Joey's backyard or in a grassy area near Caleb. She's never needed a lease though. She *wants* to stay with her family.

Cali's ears twitch. She hears my voice but sleep is demanding her attention. Pulling the truck into gear, I try get back on the main road. I haven't made much travel progress since leaving the pool grounds. Around me, loads of spectators gather on the sidewalks and police are arriving, trying to organize the chaos. All four of Kindersley's Fire Department trucks are on location, red lights flashing. An ambulance pulls up too.

Roads are blocked so I shut the truck off. It's no use. Curiosity is forcing me to say here. And not my own. I drum my fingers impatiently on the steering wheel. *I don't know what to do, God! I'm so worried about Grandpa. Keep him safe, keep him safe. Keep anyone inside safe, firefighters and occupants.*

My cell rings, making me jump. "Hello?" I jam the phone to my ear.

It's Cara. "Lyndzi! Thank God I got a hold of you. Tell me Grandpa is with you."

My heart sinks, the wolves biting at my worst fears. I shove the thought of death away, refusing to go there. "No, I was at work. Did you drop him of?"

Silence, then. "Yes, even earlier than usual. At ten-thirty."

I drop the phone, not bothering to comment. Flinging the door open, I leave Cali and run hysterically towards the fire.

A police officer attempting to keep the gawkers back grabs my waist. "Hold it! You can't go in there, miss!"

"My grandpa is in there!" I shout. "For certain! Someone needs to get him out!" I struggle to get free of his grasp but he's too strong. "Please, somebody help!"

The bald officer grabs my shoulders, looking me in the eye. "If he was at the senior's bingo event, it doesn't start until noon."

I wiggle and thrash, rational thoughts out the window as to how I will be help in a burning building. "He goes early! To look over the candy bar prize table. For motivation!

"He's not in there, miss. And that wouldn't take long to browse the prizes, he wouldn't be in there this early." I've gained the attention of the crowd. There are multiple seniors, likely on their way to bingo, standing a few blocks away. Teenagers, kids and people in work clothes gather around, whispering. Frightened. Awed by the sight of our beloved ninety year old rink roaring to destruction before our eyes. Smokey dark clouds are spiraling out of the top. The air is thick with a burning scent. My nostril tingle, as if about to sneeze. Painfully, my ears ring from the constant sound of the town fire alarm.

"You don't understand!" I shout angrily. My face is probably red and splotchy. "He goes early to pray for the residents using the building throughout the week! In the hockey bleachers beforehand!" I'm screaming now, blood boiling. I feel so helpless. "Why won't you listen? You're going to kill my grandpa!" Hot and angry tears start and sobs rack my frame.

A low male voice from behind me. "Grant, did she say someone's in there? I thought no events were scheduled yet today. It should've been locked until noon."

The officer's eyes shift to the person behind me. "Hypothetically there might be a senior inside."

"Grandpa has a key!" I yell at him, my eyes blazing like the fire eating away at the wooden structure before me. "The janitor gave it to him so he could come early on bingo days. Which is Tuesdays! Today!"

"I'm going in."

The officer releases me as a man in yellow fighter gear steps up. His dark hair is messy, his helmet by his side. The first thing notice is his skin is very tan, even for it being the middle of summer.

The officer grabs the young man, likely around my age. "Ben! I'm not sending you in there on *the chance* that there is someone in there. With the anomia from the ice machine near the fire, you could be out in seconds. Then we'd have to send someone in for you."

Unlike me, Ben has no trouble shrugging the officer's arms off him. "The fact that there is a chance someone may be stranded, is why I'm going in, Grant. I'm well aware of the dangers of this job and I don't care what's personally at stake." He shoves past the office and pulls his helmet on.

Feeling chilled, despite the intense heat from the nearby flames, I hug myself. I'm still in my dirt cover overalls and work gloves, hair in a ponytail. A mess both on the outside and inside. "God, protect that firefighter," I pray out loud, not caring at the look the officer gives me, as if God won't hear the prayers of a crazy college aged girl.

I watch Ben enter the building, mask in place, red communication gear blinking near his shoulder. His team is spraying the flames, trying to keep them at bay.

Ben disappears.

I pray more, knowing God can hear me. Knowing my sighing's are not hidden from him. I try not to dwell on the stark contrast of the black backdrop of the smoke and the spark and flame ridden building, slowing being eaten away by the intense heat.

Suddenly, Cali appears.

I bend down and pull her into my arms. For once I'm glad Emily kept the windows down. Mosquitos driving alongside us today was worth it if it meant Cali keeps me company today. She senses my distressed and paws my chest. I look into her green eyes, answering her question of the status of Grandpa.

"I don't know, Cali. I just don't know."

***

Ben:

I don't even think, aside from making sure my gear's properly on. After pushing off Grant, I briefly talk to our fire captain, Paul. He gives me the go-ahead to search the building not yet on fire for any inhabitants. "But be careful, Ben," he tells me, hosting an oxygen pack onto my pack. "If you're not out in ten minutes and we don't hear from you, we're sending in back up. To find you." His meaning is clear. Ten minutes is all I have to find the senior citizen.

Nodding, my adrenaline and training kicking in to override fear, I give my captain one final grim look. Then I slip down the face coving of my mask and step inside. Once inside hell on earth, at least from the volcano red licks of lava hot flames, that's what it reminds me off, I take a second to gather my surrounding. Every second is precious. The clock quickly ticking away.

"Greg," I say into the radio attached on my shoulder. "How's it look out there?"

Static, then: "Not good, buddy. We'll keep a steady stream going on her but hurry. She could fall within minutes."

"Roger that." My gaze sweeps over the rink lobby. The fires in the upper part of the wooden rink, to my left. For now. Even so, the air is thick with black clouds. My oxygen tank's full but if I find the elderly man, I might need to give it to him. Crawling, making myself as far from the toxic smoke, might be where this rescue mission is headed.

It's not my first fire, I've been on the squad for five years, since I was twenty-three. But this is the biggest scene. House fires have less area to cover for trapped victims. But at least the sizable rink leaves me with more areas that aren't currently on fire to search.

The woman I overheard, said her grandfather had a habit of praying in the arena around this time. *But which one?* Not liking my 50/50 odds of choosing correctly, I know who to ask. *God, show me which rink to search. I only have time to look in one!*

An overwhelming sense to turn to my right, to the curling rink furthest from the flames, comes over me. Taking it as my cure, I push open the big blue doors with my body.

Eyes frantic, my calm unravelling at the sight of five minutes left on my countdown clock, I survey the scene. *Come on, come on! Is he in here?*

Then I see a shape. Crumpled in a ball. Near the bottom of the bleachers.

I run over to him, the weight of my gear not slowing me. For once, I 'm glad for all those mandatory workout drills of swimming in jeans and sweatshirts and running sessions in our gear. Kneeling over the body, I roll him over. He's unconscious. From shock, fear of the fire alarm, falling, I don't know. There's a nasty cut on his forehead, bleeding steadily. *Best bet is he heard the alarms, smelled smoke, got frightened and fell coming down the bleacher stairs...Wait!* My breath catches in my throat.

I recognize him

He's Bradly Hollington, a senior from my grandparent's senior complex. Countless times I've joined my grandparents, Ernest and Betty Johnson, for lunch. Brady' sits at their table, always offering me a peppermint. Once I helped him fix his alarm clock and then joined him to watch *Wheel of Fortune*.

Hoisting the body up over my shoulder, I turn.

My heart drops, my knees threatening to buckle. And not from Bradley's weight.

The door I came through has collapsed. Wood beams aflame, I watch as more fall, creating a barricade. Trapping us. "Greg!" I yell into my mouthpiece. "My initial exit is covered in flames. What's the nearest exit?" I've lived here all my life but I always had hockey practice in the other rink. I don't know this smaller rink well. I don't want to waste time looking for an exit if Greg can direct me to one.

Nothing.

"Greg!"

Dark shadows, dangerous and toxic, are creeping into the arena, I set Bradly down. I check his pulse on his neck. It's slow, but definitely there. *At least he's breathing. I don't have to give him CPR.* Whipping off my mask, I give him some filtered air from my oxygen tank.

Though I don't want to, I look to the door. The entire door is gone, the wall now covered in livid fire, like hands crawling out to snatch us. All I can do now is pray to find an exit.

Because if we don't get out here soon, it won't matter if Bradly is breathing or not.

***

Lyndzi:

Hearing someone yell my name, I tear my horrified gaze from the fire. The first time in a long time. It's Emily. She doesn't say anything but wraps her arm around me. Together we watch the flames grow wider, engulfing even more of the rink. The white wood walls off the top are caving in, the metal beams the only thing left. The town fire siren has stopped but I hear police and ambulance sirens now. I bet they called in extra fire trucks and firefighters from surrounding towns.

"It's like something from a movie," Emily whispers, entranced by the fire.

"Look at all that black smoke." The firefighters are pouring water on the flames but it's barely making a difference.

Cara and Joey find us, just as the fire captain makes an announcement over the megaphone. "Kindersley is declared in a state of emergency. We need you to go back to your home. Those of you who live near, we are setting up an evaluation camp in the industry area, at the Elks Hall." He goes on to explain we can't stay here, due to something about the possibility of an ammonia leak. People around us hesitate then do what he says. But the four of us remain planted in place.

"He's been in there a long time." I say out loud, accidently squeezing Cali who give a startled meow.

Grabbing my hand, Joey bends his head. "Pray, guys, that's all we can do. It's out of our hands." So we do. With people rushing around us, back to cars, we form a semi-circle, bend our heads and pray.

For Grandpa.

For the firefighter who went in after him.

And for the fire to weaken and our town to be safe.

***

"Excuse me, but you need to leave." It's the officer again, Grant. He looks annoyed, calm, and scared, all tied in one.

I look up from praying. "Any word on the firefighter? On Grandpa?"

His faces softens. "No, I'm sorry."

Things get pretty fast paced after that.

My truck, still parked near the rink, suddenly combust into flames.

"The gas cans in the back!" Emily shrieks, as we watch our work truck completely covers in storm clouds of yellow and red embers. One spark creating a magnitude of damage. All the cars parked beside me are vacant, thank goodness. Gasping and shrieking ring out all over.

A shout to my right jerks my attention away from the truck. "He's coming out the east exit!"

"He's got the man too!" another fireman shouts, running towards a further away doorway.

Pushing aside the officer, I shove Cali into Emily's hands and run after the sprinting fireman.

The handsome looking firefighter who entered the building is no more. Face covered in shoot, coughing and stumbling, he's knees suddenly give out. Falling to the ground, his body acts as a cushion for the body he's carrying, who's wearing the fireman mask.

Dropping to my knees beside the firefighters and paramedics encircling the pair, I start to sob. I don't stop crying or even fight as arms pull me away, to let the professionals work. I'd seen what I needed too. Even in his blackened clothes and blistered skin.

The rising and falling of Grandpa's chest.

Chapter 8

"You won't relent until you have it all. Many waters cannot quench this love."

- **Lyrics from "You Relent" by Jesus Culture, my current favorite worship song.**

"How'd you get out?" I ask Ben, though I've heard the story at least ten times since it happened not twenty-four hours ago. Through live filming in his hospital room, watching accounts of it on the air, and from him telling friends and family circled around his bed. If you search, "Kindersley Rink Fire" on YouTube, someone already has a video posted. The images of the blazing fire destroying the rink sends goose bumps down my spine each time I watch it on my iPad with Ben or Grandpa.

For once, Ben and I are alone. His co-workers from the Coop lumberyard and fire crew, family, my family and the local newspaper are finally gone. I've been alternating between Grandpa and Ben's room. With Grandpa asleep, I found myself back in Ben's room Wednesday, around two in the morning.

He props himself up with his elbows. His face is red with some burns and blisters. It's mostly on his left side. "Two degree burns," is what the doctor declared. They both have some medicated salve on it now and some areas are covered in bandages. Every so often a nurse comes in to change the cloth bandages. Both Grandpa and Ben aren't in a lot of pain, due to pain medication. Grandpa described it as "Feeing like I cooked like a lobster because I forgot the sunscreen but loved the sun anyways." Both Ben and he agreed that if they don’t move too much, the raw skin on their bodies isn’t as sore. Still, even to touch them, on the damaged areas, their skin is hot to touch. You can feel the heat trapped inside, just like a sunburn.

Since burn victims metabolize faster, because of the skin healing needing extra calories, they’re going to be eating a lot more food lately. When the last nurse told him this, Ben smiled. “I have a friend who can help me with that. The guy knows how to eat big.”

“Healthy stuff and protein rich, mind you,” the fiftyish nurse told him with a smile. “Not all teen burgers and milkshakes. Though at first you’ll just want to get your calorie count up. So some of that isn’t bad. Just don’t make it your entire diet.”

“In my first year of university, I took a nutrition elective,” I told Ben when the friendly nurse left. “We all were assigned a case study and were required to draw up an appropriate meal plan for their needs.” Sitting on the bed, I arch my back. Though I’m comfy, in grey sweats, a long sleeve orange high school Volleyball tournament shirt and hair still wet from a glorious shower, thrown into a messy bun, my body feels stiff. Stress and extreme adrenaline output can be hard on the muscles. “My case study was for a burn victim.”

Ben looks up with interest. “How ‘bout that.”

“I was getting super frustrated, since the calorie requirements were so high. Like three to four thousand calories per day.”

“Man, that’s a lot! I think I usually eat around 2, 500.”

"Tell me about it." I undo my messy bun, letting my wet hair hang in loose wet waves around my shoulder. "So I started adding things like octopus sandwiches, high in protein and calorie, to fill the high caloric need."

He spits out some water, coughing. "That's disgusting, Lyndzi!"

I smirk, crossing my arms. "But it worked."

Ben pretends to pray, looking heavenward with his hands clasp. "Dear Heavenly Father, thank You ever so kindly for not making this woman in charge of my diet while I recover at the hospital."

We both laugh and share a smile. A comfortable silence follows.

The room smells like flowers and I'm sure more will be showing up tomorrow. Soon the story of "Local Boy Saves Elderly Man from Rink Fire in Southern Saskatchewan" will be in papers. And not just the *Kindersley Clarion* but in bigger ones.

Ben takes a long sip from his ice water before launching into his story. "I was all out of hope for finding an exit. The smoke was starting to get to me, in between buddy sharing with your grandpa. I felt dizzy. I told myself I would just have a little rest." He meets my eyes. "But then this warmth came over me."

"But not hot, like the fire."

He smiles at me helping to share the story. "Right. This was a pleasant warmth."

I lean forward, loving the next part. "And it energized you, clearing your head."

“And then it started to leave and I wanted it back.”

“So you followed it to a different exit, like it was a dog leading you to something.”

“Pretty much. But you and I both know it had to be an angel. Or maybe God Himself.”

“Definitely something divine. That has God written all over it.” I hadn’t realized that I had crept closer to Ben as we tag teamed sharing the story. I’m really close to him now. A part of me wants to reach out and touch his face, to feel the damage his heroic actions caused him. What saving my beloved Grandpa did. “Thank you,” I tell him quietly, realizing I’ve never actually said the words yet. In the hustle and bustle of the town being unevaluated, as the firefighters regained control of the fire, even salvaging part of it, I’d forgotten to share my gratitude.

Ben takes my hand and smiles. An adorable smile. Maybe more so then I thought yesterday, because of what he’s done. How his actions have shown his heart. Even with a burned face, you can tell he’s a good looking guy. “When I saw it was Bradly, it felt like I was saving a friend. I’m just as glad as you that we both got out okay.”

I look down at our hands. *What if...?* Could this be the start of a love story that God is writing? It certainly has an epic crossing of paths. Kindersley is big enough and I haven’t lived here long enough to know everyone, despite there not being a ton of young adults here.

Ben releases my hand and I return it to my lap. “Pretty crazy start to the work week, for all of Kindersley, hey?” he jokes, again reaching for his water. He can’t seem to stay hydrated.

"I'll say." Though Ben and Grandpa were the only injured, multiple nearby houses suffered paint damage and broken windows. After four hours, the fire finally went out. In the quick news release on CBC I watched in Grandpa's hospital room earlier, it said a total of sixty firefighters from Kerrobert, Estonia, Easton and Kindersley worked to get the fire out. As for the ammonia scare, the ice machine was found in a different location, on storage for the summer season.

"Did they ever say the cause of fire?" I ask, clicking on the sound on from the muted TV hanging on the wall.

"Arson has been ruled out. They think maybe wiring overheated and sparked something flammable."

We both watch the fire feature on the screen. There all basically the same thing they've been reporting since the fire. Every now and then new information will be shown. This one doesn't have anything about Grandpa and Ben though. It's probably a report on what happened post Ben coming out with Grandpa. I turn up the volume so we can hear the woman reporting better, standing outside the ash covered ruins of our old rink.

"Firefighters fought nearly four hours to save this rink." She gestures to the rink, half of which is gone. "Threating both the new hockey rink and old curling rink, which were attached in the middle by a lobby. Firefighters used special fire tactics to save the old rink." She turns to the fire captain. Paul's wearing a black polo with the Kindersley Fire Department crest over the heart. "Tell us what your crew did Tuesday morning, Chief Williams."

Paul, calm in the face of fire, looks very uncomfortable in front of the camera. Ben and I laugh as we watch, despite the serious topic. Standing next to the woman, most likely she's wearing mega heels, Paul small frame seems incredibly tiny. He's got muscular arms and with his black hair and round glasses, he's a dead ringer for actor Eugene Levy. "To save the curling rink, we decided to tear down the lobby and ceiling with a track hoe," Paul, explains, removing his glasses to clean them with his shirt. "Essentially, creating two separate buildings, one on fire, and one that we prevented from being contagiously set into an inferno. One of our firefighter's an operator." Paul finally makes eye contact with the camera instead of the reporter. "We got him in there and kept lots of water lines flowing in his direction, to protect him as he worked in that area. It kept those massive flames from consuming him and his machine."

The reporter and the fire chief talk a bit longer. About how the daring tacit worked, leaving some areas in tack, with smoke and water damage. Eventually it cuts to a commercial and Ben takes the remote, aims it at the small black TV and turns it off. "I'm glad everything worked out, that they could save some of the rink. This town is totally a hockey town and it brings in a lot of revenue and community spirit from it."

"Agreed."

"Lyndzi?"

I look away from the blank TV screen. "Hmm?"

"I'm glad we met." His grin turns lopsided and my heart melts. "Despite the less than ideal situation."

I match his grin and can't help the silly and infatuated smile that comes across my face. And if Emily where here, even if I could see her face, I know what'd it be.

Poker face supreme.

But hey, you never know, he could just very well be my Boaz. Someone that crossed my path at a time I wasn't expecting it. But God was expecting it all along, waiting for the opportune moment to introduce us. *Thanks for this guy,* I pray as I visit with Ben into the early hours of Wednesday morning. *I'm so glad he was written into my life story yesterday.*

My heart grows fonder for The Lord.

You are the best life and love story writer, indeed. More than qualifying for me to give You the pen and trust You to write away.

Epilogue:

You know a relationship is a good match when you don't slow your run to Jesus down because of it. Your boyfriend, fiancée, or husband, should match or increase speed of your pace and you pursuit to serve Jesus and others together in the race of live, not slowing you down. Your eyes shouldn't have to flicker from Christ to look over your shoulder. The guy in your life should be running right beside you, eyes on Jesus.

- **Emily and Brandon were talking about this concept on the way home from Blackstrap from the mud run, ever since Emily read the concept in a relationship book by Jackie Kendal.**

Ben and I end up deciding to be "just friends". Though the shared experience of the fire, we do form a lifelong friendship. We date from August until mid-December, long distance with me back in the city. But then we realize that just because we both have a Matthew 6:33 philosophy on life, to seek God's will first before anything else, doesn't mean we will make a good marriage partner. He wants to do missions work overseas, I'm a home country girl, wanting to do volunteering here, close to home. Through we're both introverts at heart, he prefers to go out in the evenings and I like to stay home. We both want kids and have similar interests, like playing guitar and spending time with family.

"Just friends," we decided, no hard feelings, hugging each other.

"Let's actually do it," Ben says into my ears. "Keep in contact."

"And keep praying for each other, as we do life separately and wait for a compatible person to marry."

Ben's eyes light up at the idea. "Prayer buddies, love it." His blue eyes stare down at me fondly. I love how he pursued me, making me feel wanted, as the famous Hunter Hays song says. His intentions were clear and he respected the standards I made about no kissing. Not a standard everyone has to make but I chose to. Though we did hold hands and cuddle while we dated. Not bad things at all, as long as you keep it PG.

Ben has some slight scarring on his left side of his face. But his tanned skin helps lesson the harshness of it. Even soot faced, stumbling from the fire, carrying my unconscious grandpa, he was attractive. Through *character* attraction. Bravery. Kindness. Selflessness. Determination.

As we both wanted, we do stay friends. And actual friends, not just the Facebook kind. We hang out in groups, go for coffee, visit Grandpa together or see a movie when we're in the same town. All the while, we remember the words of Proverbs 31:12: Keeping our future spouse in mind in how much time we spend together and how close we are, honouring them all the days of our lives.

Tomorrow is January 1st. I always reminisce about the past years trials and trumps and dream of what unexpected things could occur in the coming New Year. Usually I dwell of possible relationships. But this year I'm more content. I want it someday but I'm not longer longing for it.

I know there is reason for the waiting. My heavier toolbox with relationship wisdom, from this summer alone, testify to it. I made a far better girlfriend to Ben because of those summer conversations, interactions and lessons learned. Just think of what kind of wife I'll make with additional weight added to my tool box.

So I'll dream.

And I'll pray.

And I'll enjoy and use these unique, on a countdown, single years for God, to the best of my ability.

Yup, I'm waiting, though not always patiently. But God can help me with that.

At the sound of the car horn, I grab my coat and keys and leave. Emily and Brandon are waiting outside my condo to drive me to our church's young adult New Year's Eve party. I smile as I approach, seeing Brandon gently kiss Emily's cheek inside the car. They make the cutest pair and I'm so thankful for them in my life. We drive away to the church, to a night of food, dancing, video games and the famous New Year's countdown. We pull into the snow plowed church parking lot. I think of one more thing I'll be doing in the waiting years.

I smile but don't share when Emily questions the grin. "On a need to know basis," I ironically tell her.

In the coming season, whether two months, two years or twelve, there's one thing I bet I won't be able to resist:

Interrogating Emily, even if unsuccessfully, for more inside information ☺

Acknowledgment:

The way it works with me is God will give me the main characters name. Next the tagline, the hook that will draw people in. In this case it was the words you see on the cover, "God told her best friend who she would marry... but her friend won't tell." After that, I receive the moral of the story. Then a title. I know, this process is kind of backwards according to a lot of other authors. But it's how God communicates that He has a story He wants to write through my fingertips.

I was working at Indigo bookstore one day, ringing in a customer's purchase. I asked if she had a loyalty card with us, which she did. Taking the purple card, I scanned it into our computer. Immediately her information came to live on the screen.

Including her name.

Lyndzi.

It caught my attention, initially because of the unique spelling of the rather common name. *That would make a cool main character name,* I thought to myself scanning the barcodes of her various books and gift ware.

Suddenly, I got *that* sense.

Oh, man. Not again, God. I just finished editing the last book! And I'm still trying to figure out how to get the last several published.

But God is persistent and finally I told him okay. *Give me the story line and I'll write this down for You.* Thus, the beginning of *My Boaz, His Ruth.*

Like, Lyndzi, I'm excited for the day I'll get married. But God is teaching me that lessons are still needed to be learned *apart* before I meet that man. I prayed big things for a husband and in order to get that godly guy, God still needs time, future life experiences and interactions to work on us both.

Praying you take something away from this book, storing it away to use later or right now.

Thanks to the following books that taught be so much about relationships this year, most of which I refereed to throughout the book. I *highly* recommend you read these books. What I took away from them may not be the extent of what you individually need to learn.

The Sacred Search by Gary Thompson

Love without Limits by Nick Vujicic

Real Men Don't Text by Ruthie and Michael Dean

A Man Worth Waiting For: *How to Avoid a Bozo* by Jackie Kendall

Stay strong, reader friends! Don't settle. You won't regret not settling but you will regret if you do. In the paraphrased words of Gary Thompson in his *Sacred Search* bible study video, session 1, "You can't know what future trials you'll encounter but you *can* choose who you'll endure them with. Just as you can't foresee what success you'll be blessed with in future days but you can choose who you'll celebrate them with." Love that! Pray and let God help you make a wise choice.

I leave you with one final quote from yours truly (that I ran out of chapters to use in!): **Inspire men in your life to be godly men through the way you live *your* life. They may not show it, but they are observing you. Encourage, acknowledge, applaud and show gratitude for their godly and upright behaviors, instead of always criticising the flaws.**

Ps. Thanks to God who gave me the words for yet another tale! Use this story to bring people to You and to give people supernatural patience, quiet understanding about the necessary wait and more weight to their marriage prep toolboxes. Love You, Lord! You are so creative and kind! Thank You for this writing gift. Help me to use it to glorify You and point others not to me or my talent, but to You and Your unconditional and everlasting supernatural love.